(Mis)carriage

A mother's story of
why pregnancy loss matters

Regan Parker

Published in the United States by Saltwater Coast Publishing

Saltwater Coast Publishing

820 Fairway Rd.

Lake Oswego, OR 97034

publisher@reganparker.com

Library of Congress Cataloging-in-Publication Data is available upon request.

ISBN (Hardcover) 978-1-7339565-0-5

ISBN (Paperback) 978-1-7339565-5-0

Ebook ISBN 978-1-7339565-1-2

Book cover design by Damonza

Book editing by My Two Cents Editing and Follow the Buffalo Studio

Photography by Briana Morrison

First Edition

LETTER TO THE READER

WHEN I BECAME pregnant for the first time, I was the happiest I had ever been. I had waited so long to become a mother, and I embraced my new journey to motherhood with all my heart. When I miscarried, I was completely unprepared for what would happen to me physically and emotionally. I could not find resources to help me understand what my body would go through or what I would see and experience. I couldn't find enough support for the heartache that followed. I felt alone. I was devastated, confused, and scared. I knew that other women and families had been through a miscarriage, but I didn't find anything that told, with brutal honesty and detail, what would happen to me.

Miscarriage affects so many women and men, and I want to offer my story as a way to continue to open the dialogue around this silent yet shared experience. This is my story. It is honest, true, and raw.

I also want to provide a resource for families and friends whose loved ones are experiencing a loss. It wasn't until my family read this manuscript that they fully understood what I went through. Perhaps this book can help save someone else from suffering as long as I did. Perhaps we can finally talk about this openly and without shame. Perhaps, as has been so beautifully suggested by James Van Der Beek, among others, we can rename this heartbreaking loss. Perhaps we can finally shed light on one of the last remaining dark places in our society. This, reader, is my hope.

My baby was wanted and was planned for; even longed for. For me and my husband, from the moment we conceived, this was our baby. It was not an embryo, it was not a fetus, it was not a bunch of cells. It was our baby. And with it came all of the years of dreaming, imagining, and hoping that goes along with wanting a child.

It's important for me to note that this book is not meant to be a discussion about when life begins or whether or when women should be allowed to have an abortion. My intention is not to create a discussion around this longstanding debate.

I do not intend to speak for women who conceive unexpectedly, who may not be ready for or want a child, or who may have conceived through rape. Whatever their reasons and whatever their feelings towards their pregnancy and what is happening to their bodies, this is not a book about them.

This is a book about me: a woman who knew her entire life that she wanted a baby, and when she finally conceived, put every single ounce of her happiness into that baby.

Then lost it.

This recounting of my miscarriage and recovery is an honest and true account, and it includes very real and graphic details of what occurred. Some of the details may be difficult for some readers, but for the sake of raising awareness and empathy for all mothers and families who have encountered this same experience, I have shared mine. I am offering my story, in all of its painful and raw beauty, as a way to try to give a voice to those who suffer in silence. I hear you. I see you. I am you. I am the one in four.

For Wyatt and Hudson. I waited my entire life for you and yet nothing could have prepared me for how profoundly you would change me. In allowing me to be your mother, you have given me the greatest gift of my life.

CONTENTS

PART I

WHAT A BABY
MEANT TO ME

I HAVE KNOWN since I was a little girl that I wanted to be a mother. My parents, Tom and Joy, a captain of business with a degree in physics from Stanford and a creative, warm, and brilliant former teacher, set a wonderful example of parenthood. They were calm and patient, even when my wild nature would challenge them. They never faltered in their love and support for me—I was always welcomed with a smile, with a shoulder to cry on, and a warm embrace. Throughout my life, I always knew that I was important—who I was mattered, what I had to say mattered, and what I did mattered. It was with this strong foundation that I was given the freedom to be who I was—to pursue what made me happy, and to make mistakes.

Growing up in New Hampshire, we had a big yard, and my mom and dad spent countless hours working in the garden. Rows of peonies, roses, and tulips signaled that the best time of the year had arrived: early summer. My favorite was always the lilac bushes. Their scent was so strong that the moment I opened the door to run outside, the fragrance overtook my senses. For a few weeks every summer they overflowed with blossoms, almost collapsing under their weight. The branches somehow never gave way. Full of possibility, of potential, of beauty, they would bend to seemingly impossible depths.

If it looked like one might break from the weight of its fullness, my mom would tie it up with twine, waiting for the petals to fall off and the branch to, once again, resume its natural position. In the winters, I marveled at the lilacs' ability to weather the fierce wind and snow. They could withstand even the fiercest wind and grow bigger and stronger because of it.

Life certainly wasn't perfect, but I grew into a strong, passionate woman known for calling the shots and standing up for myself. I knew I wanted to become a mother and raise children who would be able to stand in the fullness of who they are.

I would give my children everything I had been given. Love them with the depth and passion that I was loved. Let them know they were my entire world—that my children's happiness would be my biggest, most powerful priority.

For years I marveled at pictures of beautiful pregnant women, knowing I wanted that to be me. One day I would be in full bloom with my burgeoning belly and my peace and happiness would be on display for everyone to see.

In college, I began taking care of other people's children. Being a nanny gave me a sense of peace that I struggled to find elsewhere in my life. I knew that however hard my day was, if I could take a walk by the ocean with the baby in the stroller, I would be happy. It cleared my head and made me feel like I was part of something bigger. All my stress and problems evaporated in those quiet minutes. I knew parenting wasn't always peaceful, and that sometimes the demands would be overwhelming. But deep down, I knew the gifts and magic of being a parent could bring my life full circle and give me the peace and happiness that I would not find anywhere else.

I met my husband after I graduated from law school. I had moved from Los Angeles to be closer to my parents and was living in a cottage down the street from Reed. The night we met, we both knew we were in for it. In a sea of people, we would catch each other across the room and connect with a look—both wondering why we were talking to other people and not to each other. Our wedding in Big Sur was magical. Overlooking the ocean, surrounded by flowers, the vast Ventana mountains, and our closest loved ones, we pledged to love each other through thick and thin.

When we finally decided we wanted to have a baby, I felt sure that I had prepared myself as best I could. I had lived a fun and fulfilling life. I had reached a point of satisfaction in my career, knocked a few experiences off my bucket list, and was ready to give myself over to a child.

We couldn't wait to welcome a new little person into our lives. I would finally become a mother.

GETTING PREGNANT

BEFORE WE STARTED trying, I went in to see my thyroid doctor to make sure I was clear to get pregnant. I had been managing my thyroid condition for years, and my doctor had warned me in prior visits that if my thyroid hormone levels went too high or too low, it could impact a pregnancy and baby. Too much medication and I could miscarry, too little and the baby could have developmental issues and brain damage. Once we received the okay from my doctor, we went for it. Some of our friends had had trouble getting pregnant, so we were expecting it to take a few months. It didn't. We got pregnant immediately.

They tell you not to take a pregnancy test until you are about a week late, but I had been waiting for this moment my whole life and I wasn't interested in waiting.

Many women's early lives are spent fearing a positive pregnancy test. Getting through our teens and early twenties without an unwanted pregnancy is sometimes like walking through a minefield. Some of us make it, some don't. I did, and it was great to finally be excited to see what was on the stick. I peed on it, put the cap on, and sat and waited. Sure enough, I was knocked up.

I was stunned. I didn't think it would happen so quickly. But there we were. On the journey to parenthood.

We Told Everyone

We were so excited, we told my parents immediately, and I also told my closest friends. I was elated, but also naive. It didn't occur to me that there could be anything wrong with the pregnancy. I figured getting pregnant was the hard part, and once that happened, it was all ultrasounds and shopping from there.

We had Reed's parents over to tell them, and we gave them a present of infant pajamas as our way of announcing it. They were happy, but I remember their puzzlement over the fact that we didn't have an ultrasound to show them. Reed's parents were conservative and very traditional. They were of the school that believes you wait until the second trimester to tell people, but we were so excited, we wanted everyone to know.

Blissfully Unaware

A few days in, I had some spotting and had a moment where I thought something might be wrong. Everything I read told me this could be normal, so I didn't worry too much, the thought of a miscarriage never crossed my mind. I was relatively young, I was healthy, and I *wanted* this baby, so I felt sure everything would be fine.

In a few days, the spotting let up and I coasted into the early phases of pregnancy with big, sore boobs, nausea, and cravings for meat and carbs.

Since I hadn't expected to get pregnant so quickly, I hadn't found an obstetrician yet. I did some research and found an OB nearby and booked our first appointment. To my surprise, the clinic made us wait until I was eight weeks along before they would see us, so we started the long wait for an ultrasound.

I didn't know much about the whole process of getting pregnant and seeing doctors and getting ultrasounds. I just thought you got pregnant, took a pee test, and then went in to see the baby.

At the time, I didn't understand why we weren't brought in right away to confirm the pregnancy, but in hindsight, it seems like doctors don't want to waste their time confirming pregnancies that are going to be lost.

I know now that the medical reasoning for waiting until eight to twelve weeks of gestation is that a heartbeat can't be detected until around six and a half or seven weeks—at the earliest—and that's one of the ways to confirm that a pregnancy is viable.

"The earliest you could expect to see a heartbeat on an ultrasound is six weeks," explains Dr. Robin Kalish, an OB-GYN at Weill Cornell Medical College. "Still, a pregnancy can be perfectly healthy and not have a visible heartbeat at six weeks. Many doctors are hesitant to bring a patient in that early because if no heartbeat can be found it can worry her unnecessarily. By eight weeks though, there should definitely be a nice, strong heartbeat. So [this is] the optimal time for a first appointment by many doctors."

So, hopeful, expectant parents are left to linger in a chasm of not knowing. Is it viable or not? Are they really pregnant?

Due to the high rate of miscarriage—as many as one in four pregnancies—I believe more helpful information should be provided about what to expect and what could happen during the early weeks of a pregnancy. Yes, it could worry new mothers and fathers, but if the reality is that so many of us will experience this loss, shouldn't we be better prepared for the possibility?

I went into our first appointment at eight weeks full of anticipation, excited to see my baby and hear its heartbeat. Just because I hadn't yet seen her didn't mean I didn't already love her and feel her presence in our lives. Later, I wondered if our experience reflects the experience of other couples who are subject to a medical culture that suppresses and ignores our early attachment to a baby we might lose.

I can't speak to whether losing a baby at five weeks feels any less painful and sad than a mother who loses a baby at eight or ten or more weeks, but I believe the practice of making women wait until eight weeks is condescending. It makes certain assumptions about what a new mother needs and feels about her pregnancy from the onset. Most miscarriages happen before eight weeks, so at what point did doctors and hospitals decide to reduce their chances of having to deal with women who have lost their babies?

Does the medical culture feel we won't get as attached if we don't see our babies on ultrasound screens? Or that we should more readily be able to dismiss the loss because it was during the first trimester?

When I lost my baby at eleven weeks, it felt that way to me. And when I started talking to other women about miscarriage, I learned that it felt that way to them, too. I felt like my doctors expected me to understand that early miscarriage was routine, so I should feel less sad. Whether I had seen her little body on an ultrasound screen or not, her loss was devastating. And if I had never been in to see a doctor, and experienced a miscarriage at eight or nine weeks, the physical, medical experience would still have been traumatic.

I realized that part of the taboo and silence around miscarriage is the belief that if a woman really wants a baby, somehow her desire is strong enough to protect her from losing a baby. This falsehood effectively convicts mothers for not doing enough or not wanting their babies enough.

The silence around miscarriage also implies that if a mother didn't intend to get pregnant, her attachment to her baby is somehow less meaningful, so her grief should also be less devastating.

In my experience and my conversations with other mothers, a loss is a loss. We need to allow each woman to grieve in her own way—whatever the circumstances of her pregnancy and whatever her feelings in the wake of her loss.[1]

A Heartbeat!

I wasn't told what to expect at our first appointment. I didn't know what I should expect to see on the ultrasound screen. My expectations were formed by what I had read online, which I had mostly skimmed. I just knew I would meet with a nurse

1 *A note about miscarriage statistics: The statistics on miscarriage are difficult to ascertain with any degree of certainty. Depending on when you consider a woman to be pregnant and when she loses the baby, the statistics can vary wildly. If a pregnancy is counted at the time of fertilization, some studies estimate that as many as 70-75% of all pregnancies are lost. By some estimates, as many as 30% of all embryos that are implanted are lost. Even the word miscarriage can be misleading; it is defined as the loss of a pregnancy before twenty weeks. A baby that is lost after twenty weeks is considered to be stillborn. Stillbirth accounts for 1% of all pregnancies. The most common statistic given is that 15-20% of all known pregnancies are lost to miscarriage. This means that after a woman confirms she is pregnant, but before she hits twenty weeks gestation, 15-20% will be lost. I use the one in four statistic throughout this book because I believe that it is a more accurate representation of the facts—including both miscarriage and stillbirth.

practitioner or an OB, that they would conduct an ultrasound, and that I would hear my baby's heartbeat for the first time.

Our doctor, whose name I'll omit to protect her privacy, was young, and nice enough. After confirming my pregnancy with a transvaginal ultrasound, she told me to take my prenatal vitamins and not to gain weight too fast. That was about it. She said my early spotting was probably just from my body stretching and expanding, and not to worry. A strong heartbeat was the best indicator that things were fine. I had lab slips drawn up for some blood work and scheduled a return visit for three weeks later, and we were sent on our way.

Reed and I were on cloud nine after seeing the baby and hearing its heartbeat. It was one of those moments you read about and wait for. It was just as incredible and exciting as it looks in the movies.

My baby. *Alive.* With a beating heart inside me. It was surreal.

All the medical research says that once you hear a baby's heartbeat, the chances of miscarriage decrease dramatically. Our eight-week appointment was flawless. We saw the baby, saw a strong heartbeat, and were reassured that things were going according to plan.

Maternity Shopping

After our first appointment, I felt a bit better about admitting I was pregnant to other people. I was throwing up and having a harder time fitting into my clothes. I had finally picked up some books about pregnancy, but I skimmed over the pages about miscarriage. I knew it was possible, but felt reassured by the fact that only 5% of pregnancies are lost after you hear the heartbeat. I actively avoided reading about miscarriage. I didn't want to think about it. I was worried that I would somehow curse this baby if I paid too much attention to what could go wrong. Plus, it was a real downer. I wanted to focus on being happy and excited.

I finally caved and went shopping for maternity clothes. I was a little uncomfortable trying things on because I wasn't past my first trimester yet. Part of me was nervous about buying the clothes. Looking back, I wonder if part of me knew I would lose the baby. I had a moment, standing in the changing room at the Gap, looking in the mirror wearing grey maternity pants and a tank top. Worry started to creep in. Am I really pregnant? Do I really get to do this? I had waited for this moment for so long, but in that moment, I was scared to allow myself to be excited.

I quickly pushed these thoughts out of my head and focused on finding something cute that would hide my belly for a bit longer. I remember trying on jeans with the over-belly panel and feeling *so* comfortable. I finally felt pregnant. I was excited to see what I would look like when I really filled them out. I spent more than I should have, but I figured if I had waited so long for this experience, I could justify spending a bit more to look and feel great.

THE APPOINTMENT

ON THE DAY of our eleven-week ultrasound, I dressed up and wore brand new red lipstick. It sounds superficial, but at the time, Miranda Kerr, a model and newly pregnant mom, had started wearing this bright red lipstick with minimal makeup. She looked gorgeous with an effortless beauty I associated with happiness and motherhood. The same day I bought maternity clothes, I stopped into the Aveda store and bought the perfect red lipstick—bright, summery, happy. Now, here I was—in bright red lips—ready for my ultrasound and ready to embrace my pregnant body and all that went with it. Walking in for the second ultrasound I had that glow, and the lipstick made me feel like I was exactly who I wanted to be as a soon-to-be new mom. Once we were through this appointment, I would be able to tell everyone. I imagined I would begin blossoming into a goddess-like pregnant woman with flowing dresses and red lipstick.

There's Nothing on the Ultrasound Screen

With Reed by my side, I lay on the table anxiously awaiting the doctor and the next ultrasound. I was so excited to see the baby again and get on with this whole pregnancy thing. Our doctor made some small talk and then put the transducer wand on my stomach. At eleven weeks, the baby would be big enough to see with an over-the-belly ultrasound. She searched around. The ultrasound screen was black.

We couldn't see anything. A look of concern grew on her face as she continued pressing and poking around.

Then she stopped.

"What's going on?" I asked.

"I can't find the baby with this, so we need to do a trans-vaginal ultrasound to look for it. We should be able to see it by now."

"Okay, but what does that mean?" I asked. In that moment, it began to sink in that something was wrong. Deep in the core of my being, I felt fear that I had never experienced before. With desperation, I asked, "Is the baby okay? Is something wrong? What could be wrong?"

"It could mean that it's not growing as fast as it should."

But what did that *mean*?

My mind was frantic—looking for some other explanation for what she was telling me. I desperately held back my urge to scream and curse at her. As the seconds hung in the air, I was suddenly barely able to choke out any words.

"Is it okay?"

The doctor left without answering my questions. Reed and I waited in the room alone. I began to sweat. Tears welled up in my eyes. She came back in and without saying a word, inserted the ultrasound wand into my vagina. It was cold.

She moved it around and finally, we saw something on the screen. The baby was the same size as the last time we had an ultrasound. But it looked different. It wasn't moving. Nothing was moving.

"There's no heartbeat. It stopped growing a few weeks ago," the doctor announced with finality, the wand still inside me.

"Nooooooooooooo. God, noooooooooo." The sound that came out of me was primal.

My baby was dead.

I was dead.

I'm Just a Number to You

Reed squeezed my hand. The doctor still had the wand inside of me, taking measurements. She'd just told me that my baby was dead, and I didn't even get a minute to breathe or to process what she said. I wanted to curl up in the fetal position and sob, but instead, I had to lie there, legs splayed wide open, with this woman shoving a hard plastic object around inside of me. I couldn't get up. I couldn't hug my husband. I just lay there, tears streaming down my face, waiting for it to be over.

We were told our first baby had died at eight weeks, four days. Just after our last appointment.

"I have to go get another doctor to look and confirm. I'll be right back." She left the room. I don't think she even said she was sorry.

Another female doctor came in. I recognized her from her picture online and remembered considering her as our OB, but deciding to go with this other one. What an awful way to meet her, I thought. She put the wand back inside me and poked around until she found the dead fetus. She confirmed that it had no heartbeat.

"I'm sorry," she said. At least someone said it, I thought. They both left the room and gave us some time. I was sobbing. I don't remember much else, other than just feeling dead and not being able to control myself and the tears that were streaming down my face. I stood up and struggled into my clothes.

The doctor came back in and started to explain my options. She told me I could do one of three things. I could wait for my body to expel the fetus naturally, which generally happens within about a week of the fetus no longer being viable.

"My baby's been dead inside of me for three weeks. Apparently my body hasn't figured it out yet. I'm still puking. What else?"

She then told me I could come in for a D&C, a surgical dilation and curettage procedure, which would be done in the hospital. A doctor would go in and take the fetus and tissue out. I would be done in a few hours.

Or I could go home and take care of it with a prescription.

"I want to be home," I said. "I don't want to go to the hospital." This was such an intimate experience, letting go of a baby. I didn't want to be in a medical setting. All I wanted was to get out of the doctor's office and be home.

She explained to me that I would get a prescription for misoprostol and would stick four pills into my vagina. I would then wait and my body should respond by cramping within twelve hours or so. If it didn't work the first time, I would do it again the next day with the remaining pills. If it still didn't work, I would have to come back and have a D&C.

"Fine. Call in the prescription." While she was typing in the prescription, she looked at me and made the most disingenuous sad face. It's like she suddenly realized what was happening to me, and knew that she was supposed to show some kind of empathy, but it was a face made more out of what she was supposed to do rather than actual empathy. To this day, I can't get it out of my head. It was like an overly exaggerated, patronizing frown. Like the one you give a kid who just lost his balloon. This was my baby and that's all she could manage as a response? "I hate you" is all I could hear in my head.

As I stood up and started to get dressed, the doctor packed up and started to leave the room. Then she stopped and checked my chart again. Because my blood type is RH negative, I had to be given a shot of RhoGAM so my blood didn't mix with that of my baby's. My body could start making antibodies that would harm a future baby if its blood type were RH positive, so the shot would help prevent that from happening. She walked out of the room and when she came back in, she had me pull down my pants and bend over the exam table. She gave me a shot in my butt and sent me on my way. No explanation of what to expect. No offer of support. Just a shot in the butt and a prescription. The entire experience felt inhumane.

I'm Not Pregnant Anymore

We walked out and it was obvious that I had been crying, even though I had tried for several minutes to compose myself. I remember looking at the people in the waiting room, thinking they must know what had happened.

I can't believe I wore this stupid red lipstick. I feel like a complete idiot. I had worn this Jackie O-style top and when I walked in that morning, I'd thought I looked like the most perfect, beautiful pregnant woman. But I wasn't pregnant anymore.

Reed and I had taken separate cars. He was supposed to go back to the office, and I'd planned to work from home that day. Neither of us was thinking clearly, so we didn't think to just leave a car at the doctor's office and drive home together. I had to pull myself together enough to drive. I'm sure he hugged me before I climbed into the car, but I can't remember much of it. All I could think about was the fact that my baby was dead and I had to tell my mom. Everyone who knew I was pregnant knew I was having an ultrasound that day.

It was supposed to be the appointment where you get the happy send-off into the second trimester and can start telling the rest of the world that you're pregnant. But the words that I would have to say were heartbreakingly different from the news I longed to share.

My mom was on standby for my call.

Having to Say It Out Loud

I will never forget where I was on Highway 85 when I called my mom. I was alone. I could barely speak. She was expecting a happy update.

When she realized I couldn't talk, she knew something was wrong. The silence hung in the air, both of us hoping I wouldn't say what we both knew was coming. If I just kept waiting, maybe it wouldn't be real. If I didn't have to say it out loud, didn't have to tell anyone, it wouldn't be happening.

"The baby is dead." I started choking again on my grief. "It's dead."

"What?!" she stammered, the word slipping out of her with the depth of pain and fear that I've only heard a few times before—like when we found out my grandmother had a heart attack.

"It's dead. It died three weeks ago and the baby is just sitting inside of me, dead."

I don't remember the rest of our conversation. I knew she was in shock and as grief-stricken as I was. All I could focus on was getting myself home without crashing, and the fact that I'd been carrying a dead baby around inside of me for weeks and didn't know it. She asked what I needed, but I didn't know how to handle what was going on, so I just told her I'd call her later. Reed had arrived home before me, and he helped me get out of the car and stumble through the door.

The Miscarriage

Handing Me the Pills with a Smile

REED AND I went to the pharmacy to pick up the prescription and for some reason, I went inside alone. I had to wait in line for what seemed like forever. The pharmacist was a young skinny guy who looked way too happy to be handing me such grievous pills. The pharmacy made me get a consultation since it was a new prescription, so I had to stand and talk to this smiling young man. That was the last thing I wanted to do. When I looked at him, I thought, there's no way he has any idea how much pain I'm in right now. All I wanted was to get home. I didn't want to stand in line. I didn't want to look at anyone. I didn't want to hear anyone talking. The line for the pharmacy was long, and a backup line went into an aisle with condoms and pregnancy tests—an aisle I knew all too well. I kept my head down and stared at the floor.

The misoprostol I was to take was a prescription, so I had to wait for it to be filled. When the pharmacist handed it to me, I expected to be given information about how to use it or what to expect—anything. Because the medication is used not only to induce labor and expel a fetus, but also to stop postpartum bleeding associated with poor contraction of the uterus, the pharmacist thought I was being given it for something other than to force my dead baby out of me.

He looked at me to provide the "consultation" I was supposed to receive. "It should slow down and stop the bleeding."

"Not in this case," I mumbled. I grabbed my pills and the painkillers they prescribed and left.

Once again, I'd been left to wade through this experience with no information or support. Even the pharmacist, who handed me the pills with a smile, didn't know what I was supposed to do with them. Even if I had been informed enough to know what questions to ask, I was in such a state of shock and grief, I didn't have the wherewithal to ask what to expect. Shouldn't I have been given some information? Shouldn't the pharmacist have known what I was using the pills for? Could they have a made a note when they called in the prescription to make sure that I was treated with compassion? I know there was a long line of people waiting for their medication, but I was about to lose my baby, and I needed more than thirty seconds of misinformed banter from some guy behind the counter who wanted to move on to the next customer.

Keeping Up Appearances

We went home and I changed my clothes. I had a conference call scheduled for that afternoon, and I felt obligated to attend it. My boss at the time was a nice enough guy, but not particularly sensitive. I was not about to tell him a) I was pregnant, or b) that I was miscarrying. No other option seemed to exist but to carry on with business as usual.

Because of where we are as a society, I was again made to feel like my loss shouldn't be meaningful. Certainly not meaningful enough to skip a conference call. I was blinded by pain and sadness, unable to make a compassionate choice about what was best for me in those first few hours after learning she was gone. And because of the way I had been treated by my doctor and the pharmacist, I didn't feel like my grief was significant enough to skip out on a work call.

We don't talk about miscarriage, and when we do, we act like it's not that big of a deal. According to a lot of people, it's not an actual baby at that point; it's just a fetus. And because it was still early in the pregnancy, it somehow doesn't count. It's infuriating. Early or not, that baby was real to me from the moment it was conceived. At no point in the pregnancy would I have felt better—or worse—about losing the baby. I can't speak to anyone else's experience. All I know is that I lost a baby. I didn't "miscarry." I didn't have a fetus that "wasn't viable." My baby had been alive with a heartbeat and growing inside of me. Now it was dead.

I went outside for the conference call with my boss, who was the CFO, and the bank, and lay on one of our lounge chairs in the sun. I don't remember what we were talking about and I'm sure I didn't add any value to the conversation. I doubt I said anything other than "Regan is here."

When I hung up, I started crying again, feeling traumatized by the fact that I had just taken a work call while still trying to process what was happening and what I was about to face. Why did I feel like I couldn't take any time to grieve? I planned to start the abortive process that night. It was a Friday, and I figured I would try to get through it that night or the next day. Reed and I had planned to leave for a romantic getaway for a long weekend down to Carmel and Big Sur the next day. I wanted to get it over with so we could still go on our trip.

Sparkling Water and Rosé

When we found out I was pregnant, I stocked our wine fridge with nonalcoholic drinks. Now, desperate to let alcohol numb my pain, I frantically looked for my bottle of rosé. My baby was already dead, so getting drunk couldn't do any harm, and it would help take the edge off of the complete panic I was feeling. I didn't know what I was going to do with all of those stupid carbonated nonalcoholic drinks now. I shoved aside the flavored sparkling water and pulled out a cold bottle of wine. It didn't take much to get a little buzzed. I felt better crying.

My dad happened to be driving through town on his way home from a meeting and stopped by; Mom had called him earlier. I was too much in shock to know what I needed, but once he was there, I knew how badly I needed him. Rarely do I feel like a little girl who needs to be wrapped up in her daddy's arms, but when he walked in, I crumbled into him. After I finished sobbing, we talked about the doctor's appointment and drank more wine together. He stayed for a while, but eventually had to leave to beat the traffic home. There was nothing he could do. Nothing more to say.

My mom called and I could hear the fear and sadness in her voice. She said, "I'm so sorry I'm not there." I knew she would come in a heartbeat if I asked her to, but I was surrounded by a darkness that I didn't want her to see. I did my best to keep my voice from cracking and told her I would be okay, even though I didn't believe it. I had to be strong for her. She would worry all night if she heard an ounce of fear in my voice. She stayed up all night worrying about me anyway, I found out later. She had read horror stories online about misoprostol. She was so relieved when I called her in the morning and told her it hadn't been as physically painful as I expected.

What If the Doctor Was Wrong?

After my dad left, I went into the bathroom and opened the prescription bottle. I took out four of the eight pills they had given me. As I held them in my hands, I looked at my tear-stained face in the mirror. I still had traces of that red lipstick. I was so heartbroken. I almost couldn't put the pills in. Part of me wondered if there was a chance the doctors had been wrong. What if the baby was just growing really slowly? What if there was still a chance the baby could recover? Would I be killing it? Forcing it out of me? But I knew I was wrong. The baby was gone.

My body wouldn't admit it, so I had to help it recognize what had happened. My body knew how badly I wanted that baby. How much I loved it. So it held on to her.

From the moment we found out I was pregnant, I believed that this baby was a girl. My little girl. She would be sweet and wild like the lilacs. I had dreamed of her face, of the way her hand would feel in mine. But now I had to let her go. I couldn't bear the thought that I wouldn't ever get to feel her soft skin or brush the hair off her face.

I told her that I was so sorry and that I had to do this.

Shaking, I put the pills into my vagina. And waited. It was done. Out of my hands now. I had no idea what to expect. No idea what was coming.

It's Dark, I'm Alone, and My Water Just Broke

As it grew dark, Reed made his way around to all of our neighbors' houses to tell them what had happened. In his excitement for the baby, he had decided to tell people we were pregnant. At that time, we figured we had made it past the eight-week mark with a healthy baby and strong heartbeat, so we were in the clear. I remembered how much we were reassured by the fact that there was only a 5% chance of a miscarriage at that point, so neither of us had even considered it a possibility. On this night, he went to all of our neighbor's houses, one by one, and told them it was gone. When he came back, he was noticeably more inebriated than when he had left. One of our neighbors had offered him a shot to help his nerves.

I waited for the misoprostol to kick in. I put my pajamas on and laid down in bed. I had to dig around in my underwear drawer to find a pair of granny panties so I could put on a pad. I never wore them and felt so uncomfortable. Because of the stress and the alcohol, Reed passed out while we were watching some horrible, dark movie on TV. It was not what I needed to be watching during this deeply emotional moment, going through a medical process that would expel my baby. I tried to wake him up a few times, but he was out cold. I was alone.

Suddenly, I heard a pop and it felt like something was coming out of me. Sure that I was bleeding all over, I grabbed another pair of underwear so I could change them. When I went to the bathroom, there was no blood. I was confused.

What had just come out of me?

My water had broken. I had been far enough along to have built up amniotic fluid, and now it had burst open, gushing out of me and onto my pad, pajamas and the bed. I started crying again. This was supposed to be an exciting moment, the announcement that your baby is coming. I realized that I was going through labor, but at the end of it, I would have nothing.

Pain pills eased the cramping that had begun. It wasn't any worse than a bad period, of which I'd had many over the years. The bleeding started and wasn't too heavy at first. I checked and changed my pad obsessively.

Then it got worse. I was scared. I tried to wake Reed up, but he was snoring and I couldn't get him to move. Clots were coming out of me. I went into the bathroom and sat on the toilet because the pads weren't doing enough. And then I felt *something* come out.

The mass that fell out seemed huge. It was not just another clot of blood; this was the size of a golf ball. A mass of tissue, pink and purple with stringy pieces coming from it. I had to look at it.

This was my baby.

This was my baby that I had killed.

The thoughts came at me without mercy. In that moment, still holding on to the hope that the doctor was wrong, all I could think about was the fact that I had put these pills inside of me and done this to her. That if the doctors were wrong and she was still alive, I had just killed her. My sweet baby was dead now. I just forced my baby out of my body before she was ready. And now she was in the toilet.

I pulled up my pants and sat down on the floor of the bathroom. I pulled the mass out of the water and up to the side of the bowl and just sat there and wept. I sobbed harder than I ever have before. And I kept saying *I'm sorry. I'm sorry. I'm so sorry I couldn't keep you alive.*

Saying Goodbye

I don't know how long I sat there with the mass in the toilet next to me. It could have been thirty minutes; it could have been three hours. But I finally realized that I had to say goodbye. I couldn't leave it in the toilet forever.

Part of me wanted to keep it somehow. I thought about burying it, but we were living in a rented house and I wasn't going to leave her behind when we moved. In that moment, I felt I had no other choice but to flush it. But I felt very strongly that I had to honor that baby and to say goodbye to her first.

Alone on the floor of the bathroom, I spoke to her out loud. I told her that I loved her.

I told her that I was so sorry. That I would always be her mommy.

I told her to come back to me. I *begged* her to come back to me.

And I promised that I would never forget her and never stop loving her. That I would learn from this. That I would do better.

And then I flushed the toilet. She was gone.

I couldn't bear the weight of the moment alone. With Reed asleep, I called one of the few people I knew who could help me begin to process what had just happened.

My friend Sarah was living in France at the time. She was the only person I knew would still be awake. Sarah and I met in college in a women's studies course. We connected over our sharp humor and intolerance for BS. She had been one of my closest friends, and we had weathered many storms together. I called her and, thankfully, she picked up.

Sarah had been working in the field of maternal health for years; she knew about misoprostol. She understood from a medical perspective what I was going through, which helped. She also knew me well enough to help me process my emotions and find a way to pull myself together. She listened as I talked and cried. And then somehow she managed to make me laugh a little bit. She even cracked a joke about husbands never being around for the tough shit. I was so distraught about what I was going through and being alone, and that brought much-needed levity to the situation. Once I felt like I was okay, we hung up.

The bleeding had slowed significantly and the pain pills had kicked in. I could escape into sleep for a few hours until I woke up to face another day.

THE AFTERMATH

THE AFTERMATH OF the physical experience was overwhelming, but the emotional toll was the tidal wave that drowned me.

Weeks earlier, Reed and I had booked a romantic weekend away and we were supposed to leave the morning after the miscarriage. When we found out that the baby was gone, I knew that I still wanted to go, hoping a weekend by the ocean, such a meaningful place for us, would help us start to heal. We were headed to Carmel for a night and then to Big Sur to stay at the hotel where we got married.

We drove down to Carmel and had lunch at a cute little restaurant on one of the cobblestone streets. I was relieved when we sat down and I could order a glass of wine. I needed to numb the pain. I don't know what we talked about, but we tried to keep things light and not focus on the horrible last twenty-four hours. Later that evening, we decided to watch the sunset on the beach. We took chairs and a picnic of cheese and crackers and a bottle of wine. I was still just so sad, and the tears would well up the moment I let my guard down. If I wasn't busy doing something, my thoughts would inevitably drift to the night before and the fact that I was no longer pregnant.

We talked about it a bit, and I tried to tell Reed how disappointed I was that I'd had to go through that experience alone. We cried together and held each other and watched the sun go down. We took a few pictures of the sunset, and I snapped a few of Reed sitting in his beach chair, watching the waves.

Where Is My Baby?

Later that night, back in our hotel room in Carmel, a wall of sadness hit me. It literally felt like a wall. I couldn't move past it. I couldn't get around it. It stopped me. I curled up on the bed and sobbed and sobbed. The room felt cold and harsh to me. The carpet was rough, almost dry. The comforter was old and red and green and, as I lay there crying, I remembered how much I hated those colors together when it wasn't Christmas. I fell apart and sobbed and sobbed for what must have been hours. My chest was heaving with anguish and my whole body was shaking under the weight of my pain. Reed held me and tried to calm me down, but I couldn't hear him, couldn't even see him, really. I was just alone with the confusion. Why? Why did I lose her? What did I do wrong? Where *was* she? Everything that I had ever wished for, ever hoped for, everything I had waited for and planned for, was gone.

After losing a baby to miscarriage, many people experience the different stages of grief. Pregnancy hormones coursing through a woman's body can compound the sadness, anger, and guilt. According to the American Pregnancy Association, I had moved into the anger/guilt/depression stage. My feelings and thoughts were all typical for someone experiencing a pregnancy loss, but because I hadn't been given any of this information, I stumbled through these phases alone and not knowing if they would ever pass.

I don't know that I have ever cried so hard for so long in my entire life. I have been fortunate not to have lost many people close to me. When my grandmother passed away about a year earlier, it was incredibly painful. She was such a bright light in our lives and her absence was palpable. She was ninety when she died, and while it didn't lessen the pain, I could at least think about what a joyful, long life she'd had and take comfort in knowing that she knew how loved she was. When we learned of her heart attack, I drove to the hospital to be by her side. Knowing how much she loved her garden, I put a pink rose in my hair and sat by her side until we could take her home. Before the ambulance pulled into the driveway, I had gone to the florist and bought hundreds of flowers so that she would be surrounded by them as she passed. I had done my best for her, and felt comfort in knowing that she would go peacefully, surrounded by love and her beloved garden.

I knew my grandmother's heart, knew her soul. I had gotten to learn who she was and what made her happy—living by the ocean, working in her garden, listening to the birds that came to sit outside her window. I knew her face, her hands, her hair. What I struggled with for so long was the idea that I didn't get to know my baby. I would never know what made her smile or what her sweet little hands would look like. Our baby didn't get a chance to become the little girl that I imagined she was. I was plagued with wondering whether she knew she was loved. Whether she knew how much she meant to us, even for just those few weeks that I had her.

I could not come to terms with the fact that she didn't get a chance. She didn't even get the chance to be held in her mother's arms. She didn't get to feel me hold her. I've heard that some women who lose their babies later in their pregnancies hold their baby and mourn them while cradling their little body. Some have burials and ceremonies to honor them. I wanted that for my baby. I would have done that for her if I had known better. But I didn't know what to expect, didn't know what would happen to my body or to my heart.

I was completely unprepared for what I experienced in the bathroom the night I lost my baby. My doctor didn't tell me that my water would break or that I might be able to identify my baby's dead body when it came out. It was like I wasn't supposed to notice. The baby was almost nine weeks along, I had seen her little body and her heart on the ultrasound. And I was supposed to just flush her down the toilet? Or perhaps if she had come out when I was wearing a pad, I was supposed to throw her in the trash? I will be forever grateful that I followed my maternal instincts in that moment and at least took a moment to pause and look at her, to say goodbye. I can't imagine the guilt and pain I would feel if I hadn't even done that.

But why hadn't I been prepared for that moment? Why hadn't I been told what I might see or how I might feel? Why wasn't I given some guidance for how to say goodbye? I was treated like a number, like losing my baby was routine—left to flush her like she didn't matter. Perhaps if I wasn't so far along this might not be so heinous an idea, but I will forever be plagued by what I experienced that night in the bathroom and what I did to her. I didn't get to peacefully help her come out and then, with a mother's care, give her a final resting place. I wasn't in a home that was mine, or one that was hers. I knew that I didn't want to have her removed in a medical procedure in a doctor's office, but I didn't realize that I would be forced to decide what to do with her body after she had already fallen into a toilet. This house was transient, but my loss wouldn't be. If I had understood what that would mean for my grief, I would have made a different choice.

And so I never got to hold her. Never got to feel my little baby's body wrapped in my arms, or even in my hands. I was consumed with the thought that the last thing she would feel from me was my hands pulling her dead body up the side of the toilet to look at her before flushing her down. How could she know I loved her if that's what I did to her?

What kind of mother was I?

And what kind of a society do we live in that this is supposed to go unnoticed? That I wasn't meant to do anything other than carelessly disregard her brief, sparkling light in my life and treat her like she was medical waste? How can we expect a mother to do that to her baby? Is it because I wasn't yet a mother? In our society, at what point would I actually become one? When she was born? When I was past the first trimester? When? And until that point, was I not supposed to care for her or be impacted by her loss? If I was not a mother, then this wasn't a baby, and flushing her wasn't so egregious. But I was a mother, and she was my baby. And now here I was, empty. She was gone.

Her beautiful little spirit was created in my womb—a place where I protected her and helped her grow for weeks. Yet I wasn't given the courtesy of deciding how to let her go. Shouldn't I have been given a choice? Perhaps I would have been spared the years of shame and guilt if I had been able to honor her loss and to grieve her. Instead, not only was I facing the tremendous pain of losing my baby, I was also now being crushed under the weight of the shame I felt for how I treated her in the end. She deserved more. And so did I.

If I had known better, I would have taken her sweet little body and buried it in my parents' garden, under the lilac bushes.

Even though she wouldn't grow up and be my wild daughter, at least I would know that every summer I could catch a glimpse of her in the blossoms, knowing she would always be with me.

Not the Appropriate Place for Grief

As part of our romantic weekend, we had booked a night at the hotel where we were married in Big Sur; it is one of the most beautiful, peaceful places I've ever been. Perhaps there, I could find some sense of relief. The next morning, we left Carmel and drove down the coast to Big Sur to Ventana Inn. After we checked in to the hotel, we went down to the lobby and grabbed some of the wine and cheese they were serving for happy hour. We took plates outside and sat down at the tables outside the front entrance. The first glass went down quickly. I sent Reed back in for a second, maybe a third. I sat there, numb. Every half hour or so my eyes would well up with tears and I would fight to hold them back again. After a few glasses of wine, I couldn't anymore. I was distinctly aware of the other guests around me and didn't want to make them uncomfortable. I imagined many of them were there for a romantic weekend, and they certainly didn't need to see some woman crying into her glass of wine. It wasn't an appropriate place for grief.

We walked up to our room and Reed comforted me on the bed. I think we were both feeling the need to connect with one another and the wine had helped us relax a bit. We started making love and it was fine at first, and then awful. During our last appointment, our doctor had told me not to use tampons and to abstain from having sex. She hadn't explained why, so I hadn't put much stock in it. I realized very quickly why you are not supposed to: I was still bleeding fairly profusely and it felt like an open wound. We stopped; I showered and put on underwear and a huge pad. We went to dinner and then I collapsed once again into the safety of sleep.

When I woke up the next morning, I was still bleeding heavily. I was passing large clots and began to get scared. We were pretty far away from medical services, let alone a hospital. I managed to find a place on the hotel property with cell reception and called the doctor's office. They told me to take some ibuprofen and to go see them if the bleeding didn't slow down. After the Advil kicked in, the bleeding began to taper off, and we packed up our bags to go home.

The Follow-Up Appointment

A follow-up ultrasound awaited me upon my return home. I had to go back to make sure that "everything had passed"—i.e., check to make sure no parts of my baby were stuck inside of me. Literally the last thing I wanted to do was to go back to that office. Ever. But here I was in the same place I'd received my terrible news, walking in those same doors. This time, grief-stricken. A distinct change from the naive elation I'd felt the last time I walked through them.

I don't remember much from the appointment, other than having another transvaginal ultrasound wand shoved inside of me. I was given the all-clear. There was a small amount of tissue left, but I was told it should pass in a few days. I was advised to wait a few months before trying to get pregnant again, and I was sent on my way.

No mention of what to expect, no offer of counseling, no mention of a follow-up call to see how I was doing, no information given to me at all. This was routine for the clinic. With so many women losing their babies, I don't think the medical staff had a protocol in place or saw a need to let me know what to expect as I left their office. As I walked back through the double doors and into the parking lot, I vowed never to go back there again. I hated that place, the memory, the experience, the doctor.

A FEAR OF DEAD BABIES

NO ONE LIKES to talk about dead babies. A shroud of silence surrounds miscarriage and stillbirth, making the experience so much more painful and isolating. Dead babies scare people at a primal level, and I think the concept is so difficult that we have just decided not to talk about it. Even women who have gone through a miscarriage don't talk about it in much detail.

After my miscarriage, I talked about what happened with any woman that I knew had children. I'd ask whether they shared the same experience. I was shocked when so many of them admitted yes. But I found that even when I asked, and even when they would tell me yes, they still would not *really* talk about it. "Oh, I miscarried between my two girls." Or "Yes, I miscarried early before I had my son." But what did that *mean?* What *happened?* How did you feel? How did you get through it? Was your baby dead inside you for weeks? Were you still throwing up even though your baby was dead inside of you? Had you seen the heartbeat?

Did you pull the fetus out of the toilet?

These were all of the horrible questions I desperately wanted to ask and have answered, but no one wanted to talk about it. If you've experienced it, you just want to forget that it happened and move on. And if you haven't, you don't want to be scared off by talking about it. It's a horrific topic. I was left alone with my own thoughts and emotions, drifting away into depression.

When I ask other women how they overcame the sadness and devastation and fear, their answers are resoundingly the same:

Another pregnancy.

Women are moving on and covering their pain with another baby, or they are stifling their pain so far down that they can't even recognize it anymore. Not a single woman I talked to knew how to help me deal with the excruciating pain I was feeling. Why?

Because no one wanted to talk about it.

None of us knew how to talk about it.

In medical terms, I had suffered a miscarriage. But for me, as a mother, my baby had died. This is not an easy thing for anyone to talk about.

We Don't Talk About It

I am someone who needs to talk through things to process them. In the early days after I miscarried, I needed to talk about what had happened, in detail and with brutal honesty. No one really wanted to hear about it, but I couldn't stop myself.

One of my friends had welcomed a new baby into her life just a few weeks before I lost mine. I remember going to visit her and to meet her baby; I unloaded on her. I stopped by after work and had a glass of wine and kept saying, "My baby was dead inside of me for weeks." That was all I could focus on.

When I talked about it with others, I couldn't say "I miscarried" or "I lost the pregnancy." Those words didn't feel right to me. They didn't tell the true story of the horrific experience, and they didn't honor the fact that I lost a baby.

I was unable to be polite or appropriate. I was watching these friends with a brand-new baby and I was devastated. I felt robbed of that experience. I remember looking at the husband's face while I was talking about it, and he was horrified. I am sure he was wishing I could find a way to filter what I was saying, but I just couldn't. Later I would realize that I shouldn't have to. I shouldn't have to feel like I couldn't talk about it.

We Don't Know Why It Happens

Part of what plagued me about losing the baby is that I didn't know why it happened. For something that nearly a third of expectant women experience, there is a surprising lack of insight into the causes. I am someone who struggles with control. I like to be in control of things that are happening in my life, and when I feel like things are hectic, stressful, or anxiety-producing, I cling to the idea of control to ease my discomfort. To not know the cause of such a profound loss was incredibly debilitating.

We don't know why most miscarriages happen.

Even for women with recurrent miscarriages, nearly 75% of them will never know why. Why is that? Why don't we want to find out?

I was told by well-meaning friends and read in some of the literature about miscarriage that "sometimes these things just happen," or that it was "nature's way" of weeding out a baby that would have problems or would not have survived because of chromosomal abnormalities. Is this supposed to feel like mercy? That somehow I was spared some later heartbreak because she died before she was born? That a child who would be born with a disability or challenges can simply be discarded? I didn't believe this. I would have loved my baby regardless of her circumstances.

If sometimes these things do "just happen," why doesn't that spark outrage or curiosity? Would we say that to someone who died from another unknown cause? Would that person's life somehow be less meaningful?

Much of the medical information caveats the explanation of a miscarriage with "While we can't know for sure…" Because most miscarriages happen early in a pregnancy, the assumption is that there is a chromosomal issue with the developing fetus; absent any obvious issues with the mother's health, this is considered the cause. I can understand saying to a mother, "Sometimes these things just happen" or "We can't know for sure" if her child gets a bruise from a fall, or a skinned knee, or a splinter. But for its death? You would never say that to a mother about the death of her baby. But this is what women are told.

Imagine how many women are being told that today. Even in one of the most well-known resources, *What to Expect When You're Expecting*, the explanation women are given is that "a miscarriage is simply biology's way of ending a pregnancy that's not going right."

This is an outdated and irresponsible thing to say to women. Are we supposed to feel comforted by "simply" losing a baby? My baby "wasn't right" so I should feel relieved? If I don't feel relieved or comforted by this explanation, am I overreacting?

Should I not grieve? What kind of tangled mess are we leaving for women when we dismiss their pain?

Doctors are bound by the duty to inform and the duty to disclose the consequences of treatment. They are also obligated to perform in a manner consistent with the skill and knowledge of others in their field. If it is standard practice in the field of maternal health and pregnancy to let a miscarriage go undiagnosed, to offer the simplistic explanation "We can't be sure" in response to a miscarriage, and to send women home with little information or resources for support, then my doctor surely didn't commit malpractice. But even so, didn't my doctor fail me? Hasn't the obstetric and childbirth community failed all of us? Shouldn't the loss of a baby—at any stage—be treated as significant, meaningful, and worthy of a higher standard of care?

There are different models of care in other countries and here in the U.S. that handle miscarriage differently. Midwifery and alternative medicine handle the loss and trauma of miscarriage much differently than in most traditional medical clinics. Should we use those models as guides for how to better support women?

Perhaps the unknown cause scares doctors as much as it scares the rest of us. But if that's the case, we should push through that fear and give women the courtesy of inviting them to decide how to go through the process of miscarriage. Even if the outcome is to be told, "We can't know for sure, but if you'd like to try to find out, here's what we can do."

Give me the choice, as the mother of this little baby who has died, to decide what I want to know and how to grieve and say goodbye. I deserve to have a choice.

My miscarriage could have been due to chromosomal issues, or my thyroid condition, or the antibiotics I was given for an infection. It could have been *anything*, but I was never going to be able to know. I would never have an answer. Without access to any real answers, I was left feeling like it was somehow my fault.

So, not only did I have to deal with the pain of losing the baby, I had to also come to terms with never knowing why it happened. And for someone who feels better when fully informed and prepared like I do, that meant I couldn't know how to prevent it from happening again. If I knew why it happened, maybe I could do things differently the next time. Instead, I just had to sit with the fear that I was completely helpless in preventing this kind of loss and immense pain from happening to me and my family again. If I wanted to get pregnant and have a baby, then I had to deal with that possibility.

I wasn't told by my doctor why my baby died, so in the absence of an explanation, I tried to figure it out for myself. I needed to know what happened to *my* baby. Why did *my* baby die?

I found out after the fact that I could have taken in the "tissue" from my miscarriage and had it tested. That wasn't explained to me when I was in my doctor's office. I flushed mine down the toilet because no one had informed me. I will never definitively find out whether there was a chromosomal abnormality.

I began to think back. What happened when I was eight weeks pregnant? At my eight-week appointment, I saw a healthy baby with a heartbeat, so in my mind, I had to find out what happened between that day and the four days later when my baby died. Or what could have contributed to her death even earlier than eight weeks. Slowly, I pieced together what might have caused my baby to die.

What Happened to Mine

During my pregnancy, I went in for my eight-week appointment for the usual battery of tests. My doctor called to tell me that I had Strep B in my urine and probably had a bladder infection. She recommended taking antibiotics to clear it up.

I trusted her as an OB; I didn't think there was any danger in following her medical advice. As I researched into issues of miscarriage, I learned that antibiotics can cause miscarriage. Had I known that, I never would have taken them.

Months later, while in Maui and actively trying to get pregnant again, I had a bladder infection. I called the clinic and was connected with the doctor who was on call that day. He happened to be my husband's primary care physician and was a young, vibrant doctor that Reed really liked. I felt instantly comfortable with him, but was anxious about the risk an infection might pose to a possible pregnancy. I told him I wasn't sure whether I was pregnant and I didn't want to risk it by taking anything. He agreed that it wasn't worth the risk since I didn't have a positive urine culture for an infection.

I was still riddled with grief and guilt, so I asked him, "Is there a chance that taking the antibiotic when I was pregnant caused me to miscarry?" He responded, "We can't know for sure, but based on the numbers I'm seeing on your chart from then, I would not have put you on antibiotics given that you were pregnant."

Reed and my parents had just sat down at the Hula Grill for lunch. I remember sitting on the bench outside the host stand and welling up with tears. I sobbed as the reality of what the doctor had said sank in.

I thought for sure that was the answer: My first OB had made a mistake in prescribing the antibiotics and this gross oversight had killed my baby. And the worst part was that I had allowed it. I hadn't done enough research. I hadn't pushed back on taking the antibiotics. I hadn't stood up for myself or my baby. I'd followed her advice, and it killed my baby. Protecting my baby was my number one job as a mother, and I had failed.

Later, I reflected further on my eight week appointment. Along with the possible bladder infection, I had also found out that my thyroid hormone levels were off. My thyroid doctor had prepared me for that possibility and had advised me to monitor my symptoms closely so we could adjust my medication if we needed to.

The blood work done at my eight-week appointment showed that I was getting way too much medication. My thyroid hormone level was barely detectable.

My thyroid doctor told me that we should gradually back off my medication and the numbers would level out. When I saw the number, my instinct was to back way off immediately to get myself right-sided. I didn't want to do it slowly, because I didn't want to risk my baby. My numbers were so low that a miscarriage was certainly possible. Instead of fighting to do what I thought was best, which was to get my number back up as quickly as possible, I followed my doctor's advice.

In my desperation to find out what happened, I thought back to my thyroid and was consumed by shame and remorse. I hadn't fought for what I knew was right for my body. And for my baby. I hadn't even pushed back. My instincts were telling me something different, but I had quieted them to follow my doctor's orders. I had never been pregnant before, and I believed that I should trust the experts to handle the issue. I had failed again.

I will never know what role, if any, my thyroid or the antibiotics played in losing my baby, but I learned a painful and valuable lesson. As a mother, I had to trust my instincts. I had to do what *I* believed was best. No matter who was telling me differently, or the consequences, hurt feelings or anger. I learned that being a mother was fighting for your child in the face of all of it. The stakes are too high not to.

Returning the Maternity Clothes

One of the toughest moments for me in the aftermath was returning the maternity clothes I'd bought. I was so happy and filled with excitement and hope when I bought them. Now I felt dead inside.

The thought of going to the mall and returning the clothes made me physically sick, but I didn't want them in the house, just sitting there, symbolizing what was lost. I wasn't pregnant anymore and I didn't know if I ever would be again, so I certainly didn't need a bag full of clothes to remind me.

But what if they told me I couldn't return something? That too much time had passed or something was on final sale and couldn't be returned? I was terrified as I went to the counter at the Gap and handed everything over. I couldn't look the salesperson in the eyes. I just prayed they wouldn't ask me any questions.

I could feel my body fill with rage at the idea that I might have to explain what had happened. What would I tell them? My baby died, so I don't need these anymore? I wasn't a good enough mother and now I'm not pregnant anymore? I was worried that if they tried to push back on the returns I might snap.

Thankfully, the clothes were taken back without hesitation. If it's not a company policy, it should be—anytime someone tries to return a maternity or baby item, just let them. No questions asked.

Don't make someone explain their pain and grief. In the midst of the turmoil of a miscarriage, we are just not capable of having to explain or argue about a return. Just know that it's probably hard enough to stand there and hand the sweet baby clothes over. Just walking into the store breaks our heart, so please don't make it any harder. We don't know, in that moment, if we can bear any more.

I will say that I kept a few pieces of the maternity clothes. A very small part of me held onto a bit of hope that I might someday need them again.

DESPERATION

IN THE AFTERMATH and the weeks following the miscarriage, I started to feel desperate to get pregnant again. The doctor told us to wait a few months so my body could adjust and get back to normal. I didn't think she knew what she was talking about, and she certainly didn't know how much pain I was in. The thought of waiting that long just didn't seem possible. Every single day was agonizing.

When I say desperate to get pregnant, I mean literally desperate. Desperate to have something to be happy about. Desperate to erase the pain. Desperate to put it behind me, to get to a place where I could look back at it and not feel the devastation. Not feel so raw anymore. I knew that if I could just get pregnant again, I would be okay. I could move forward.

As soon as I got my period again, about six weeks later, I wanted to start trying. I talked to my friend Sarah and, in the midst of my grief, mentioned to her that I wanted to get pregnant right away. Coming from a place of compassion, she strongly advised me to wait. Based on her experience in maternal health, she said it would be better for my body to have time to heal, and I would have a better chance at a successful pregnancy the next time. I was sitting in my car in the same parking lot where I had picked up the misoprostol, and I remember listening to her and thinking, "But you just don't understand. You have no idea what this feels like. You have no idea how desperately I want to erase the pain and have a baby." There was no way she could understand. She hadn't been pregnant and hadn't suffered a miscarriage. Rational discussions went out the window.

No one could tell me what was best for me. I knew that what was best for me was to get pregnant again and have a baby.

The Two-Week Wait—I Failed Again

Reed and I began tracking my ovulation with fertility indicator sticks. I wanted to give myself every chance I could to get pregnant. I would see the happy face on the stick that meant I was ovulating, and we would go for it, consistently, every day during that window. And then the waiting began. The two-week wait.

Every little thing that could be a sign I was pregnant became an obsession. Did my boobs hurt? Was that spotting implantation bleeding? Did I feel heavier? Was that subtle pain in my uterus implantation? I went to the bathroom countless times and wiped over and over again to see if there was any spotting. Hoping for pink implantation bleeding, which I believed was the best sign that I was pregnant. As the days wore on, I began to fear seeing any red. The brown spotting would start. *That could be implantation bleeding, but it could also be my period. My boobs are definitely swollen and achy. I could be pregnant. But it could also be my period.* The symptoms are so similar, and because I was so desperate, I read into anything I could to tell me I was pregnant.

Until it became clear that I wasn't. The bleeding turned from brown to red. My period started. I failed again.

For months and months we tracked my cycle. We watched for signs of ovulation and later of pregnancy. Every month, I watched like a hawk for signs that I was fertile, and then the waiting began.

No one tells you that after you lose a baby, getting pregnant again becomes an obsession. Literally nothing else matters. I didn't see anyone or anything, didn't hear anything other than my constant inner dialogue about whether I was pregnant. Everything else was a blur, distracting me from what I cared most about—a new baby. I was so certain that getting pregnant again would erase my pain. It seemed to have helped the other women I had talked to. They barely talked about their miscarriages, so it must be that getting pregnant again and having a baby takes away the sadness. All I wanted was to not feel the devastation that had become the compass of my life. I was in limbo—not pregnant, not a mother, just waiting. Surely the excitement and happiness I felt when I first became pregnant would wash away these dark, lonely moments.

We got pregnant immediately the first time, and I expected that to be the case again. So when month after month nothing happened, I began to panic. I was in a constant state of anticipation, then would cycle through hope, fear, and disappointment. Month after month.

Getting my hopes up. Reading into every sign, secretly hoping, despite all indications to the contrary, that this time it had worked.

It didn't.

And on and on it went for nine months.

I tried everything I could to enhance my fertility. I bought bee pollen and all kinds of other herbal supplements. I started drinking whole milk, thinking the extra fat would make me more fertile. I would sit and Google fertility-enhancing foods and then go stock up on them. Most of them were disgusting, but I powered through in the hopes they might work.

Nothing did.

I now know that I was not alone in feeling like this. Many women and families become desperate to get pregnant again after a loss. According to the nonprofit organization Project Sweet Peas, "There is no greater tragedy for a parent than losing a child. It is the loss of a dream and the vision of a perfect family. When the dream ends, the need/hunger to be pregnant again is overwhelming, and sometimes all consuming... not to replace the baby who was lost, but to fill an aching void... with the hope of finding peace and purpose."

That's all I really wanted—to be a mother. To hold a baby in my arms, and to stop the never-ending anguish of losing her.

Everyone I See Is Pregnant

When you've lost a baby or are trying to get pregnant, it feels like every person you see is pregnant. The fall after I lost the baby, I went to visit one of my best friends, who was pregnant. Heather and I have been best friends since we were little. She came on our family vacations and we had sleepovers nearly every night during middle and high school. We grew up together and could be our quirkiest, weirdest selves around each other. Our husbands often joke that they don't understand our language when we get together. She's that friend who knows me inside and out, who has supported me through heartache, and who allows me to relax and be completely myself. Heather found out pretty late that she was pregnant, missing the signs for almost her entire first trimester. When I saw her, it was so wonderful to see her glowing and her belly starting to show. But it was also incredibly painful. The jealousy I felt was intense. I didn't have any ill will towards her, but I was so envious of what she had—a healthy baby growing inside her.

She hadn't bought many maternity clothes at that point, so we went to look for some together. I was happy to be with her for that milestone even though it brought back my own painful experience. The store had fake belly pillows that help moms imagine how clothes will look at the second and third trimester. We joked around as she put the pillow under a shirt to see how huge she would look—which we found awkwardly funny. I wanted in on the jokes, so I tried on some pants and a shirt and shoved that pillow in there. We were laughing and having fun, but part of me was dying. I was so happy for Heather, but so horribly sad for myself. When Heather turned around to take off her shirt, I caught a glimpse of myself in the mirror. I instantly felt sick. I was supposed to have that moment of being really pregnant and bursting out of my maternity clothes, but not with a pillow. I felt the tears well up and the wind being knocked out of me, but I quickly pulled the pillow out and turned away so Heather wouldn't see my face.

Fertility Drugs

I came home from that visit determined to get pregnant again, but now I was worried that it might never happen.

That I'd had one opportunity to have a baby and I failed.

The emptiness and guilt multiplied with every period. After nine months and seeing myself in the mirror with Heather, I decided to find a new OB. I was ready to explore all of my options—even if it meant fertility drugs and treatment.

According to a study titled "Depression and Anxiety Following Early Pregnancy Loss," anxiety, the desire to conceive again, and doubts about future fertility are quite common. The study states that "Contrary to popular belief, becoming pregnant again is not a protective factor against depression or anxiety. Mood symptoms following a prenatal loss do not always resolve with the birth of a subsequent healthy child." My deep desire to become pregnant again was normal, but the idea that a new pregnancy and baby would fill the void inside me was misguided. Even so, it is the coping mechanism for countless women. What I would later learn, and would be reminded of countless times over the years, is that I thought I could mend my borken heart with *a* baby. What I didn't realize was that my heart was broken over *this* baby. No other child could replace her or fill the hole that she has left in my heart. This doesn't diminish the complete, unbridled love I have for my two sweet boys, but she was her own spirit, and her loss still lives on in my body and in my heart.

I chose a new doctor at a different medical facility so I wouldn't have to worry about seeing the doctor whom I held responsible for the pain and suffering I was experiencing from my miscarriage. The office was far away from where I lived, but it was worth the drive. I knew I wanted to deliver at Stanford in case any complications arose. Having access to some of the best care was paramount to me and a new baby, so my husband and I chose to deal with the longer drive.

Reed and I went in to meet the new OB and talk about our fertility struggles. Our new doctor was another younger woman, but I found her to be more seasoned than our last one. She was more calm and seemed to understand the nuances of medical care and compassion. Luckily, I was considered of advanced maternal age, so after six months of trying and not getting pregnant, she could go ahead and start testing me to find out what was happening. She did blood work on me and a semen analysis on Reed's sperm and everything looked fine. I'd had bleeding midcycle since the miscarriage, but she didn't seem concerned.

After the battery of tests revealed nothing was obviously wrong, we went in for a follow-up and to discuss our options. Our doctor started to tell us about intrauterine insemination, fertility drugs, and IVF. She said we could wait and continue to try for a few more months, but I had made up my mind before even going in to see her. I asked her for Clomid, a fertility-enhancing drug, despite my fear of having multiples. I was ready to be pregnant again and I didn't care how it happened. I just wanted to move forward and have a baby.

I filled the prescription that day and was ready to start taking it. I had to wait until after my next period, so I had a few weeks to decide if I really wanted to do it. I had some reservations—I was terrified of having twins—but my drive to get pregnant ASAP outweighed my fear.

At one point, though, my mind drifted to Jen and Miranda, the Chinese Medicine practitioners who helped me when I first got pregnant, and I thought maybe I should ask them for help before taking the Clomid.

One Last Chance

The month before my first pregnancy, I went to an acupuncturist to get myself as spiritually and physically healthy as possible. I found Six Harmonies Traditional Medicine online and felt an instant, deep connection to the women who ran it.

Miranda had been an archaeologist before she began practicing Chinese Medicine. She had greying hair and a wisdom that seemed to be steeped in a well-lived life. Jen was closer to my age and despite coming across as fun and carefree was deeply intuitive. Her training and her ability to connect and read people made her a powerful healer.

My first session was with Jen, and it was relaxing and soothing. I felt good that I was centering and readying myself for a baby. Very soon after that session, I became pregnant.

I went back weeks later, after my eight-week checkup, blissfully ready to enjoy a session as a glowing pregnant woman. It was evening, after work, and I remember the room being dark. Jen talked to me about how I was feeling and then had me lie on the table to check my pulses. As she let go of my right wrist, she said to me, "Be sure to check in on your thyroid." There was quite a bit of concern in her voice, but I had already been working with my thyroid doctor to get back on track, so I wasn't overly concerned. I brushed the conversation aside and focused on enjoying my healthy baby and expanding body.

In the days and weeks after I lost the baby, that conversation with Jen and the memory of her gently dropping my wrist haunted me. Did she know? Did she know my baby was dead? Could she tell? I remember she had told me that you could usually feel the baby's heartbeat in the mother's wrist. Could she feel it before and then it was gone? Did she know and just didn't want to tell me? Was her telling me to check my thyroid her way of making sure I would go find out that my baby had died? I was so horrified by the idea that she knew that I didn't go back to see her again. To be honest, I was scared. I was scared by the idea that she could have known. That she knew and I didn't.

It was only in November of 2012, after trying to get pregnant again for nine months, that I surrendered and went back to see her. I was desperate, and deep down, I knew she could help me.

I didn't get up the courage to ask her whether she knew my baby had died or what she meant when she told me to check my thyroid until probably a year later. When I finally gathered the courage to ask her about it, she said she didn't know that the baby was dead, but she knew that something was very wrong.

I'm glad I went back not only to face my fear, but also because she ended up saving me. She helped me get pregnant again.

When I met with Jen that morning in November, I remember sitting in the room and telling her very matter-of-factly, "You've got one cycle to get this done. I'm taking Clomid next month if this doesn't work—so do your magic." She was a bit daunted by the timeline, but she also knew that I wasn't kidding.

I started crying when I told her about visiting Heather. She asked me how I felt about my visit with her and I said, "I'm jealous." She responded, "Well, let's get you pregnant."

She put me on the table to start my treatment, and it immediately brought up all of my fears. All the fears I had buried in my determination to get pregnant. What if I never get pregnant again? What if that was my one shot, the one time I got pregnant? And I lost the baby. How could I ever live with that? What if the miscarriage was caused by something I had or hadn't done, and that was my one chance? How could I ever move past that? How could I ever forgive myself? I didn't have a way to move through those fears or to find any answers, but just voicing them helped calm me down.

Jen was concerned about my midcycle bleeding, and after examining me, she said I was running hot. I needed to cool down to get my body back in balance. She treated me and gave me some strict diet guidelines: no more hot sauce (which I had been craving and eating like it was going out of style), only cooling foods, and I had to do a mung bean cleanse. I followed her advice to the T and went back in for a craniosacral session with Miranda a few weeks later.

Reed and I had been diligently having sex after my hormones started to peak and I was in my ovulation window. My new OB had suggested that I get an ultrasound to confirm that I was ovulating. I went in and the tech said she could literally see the egg about to burst out of my ovary.

There was a full moon the morning of the day I was supposed to ovulate, so I woke Reed up 6:45 in the morning and convinced him to get intimate with me, believing it might be a sign. Later that morning, I went for my cranial session with Miranda.

During craniosacral sessions, your energy is moved around to heal and reconnect you to your body. I found them to be very powerful experiences and felt that Miranda had a way of really connecting to me. We would often talk about our sessions afterwards and I would tell her what I'd been feeling or thinking about, and she would often be experiencing the same images or thoughts.

The morning before the cranial session, I had cramping to one side, and I really believed I could feel myself ovulating. During the session with Miranda, I focused on visualizing the sperm traveling up to meet the egg. It was one of the most powerful and spiritual sessions of my life, and I knew deep down that I was going to be pregnant.

Pregnant Again

THE NEXT NIGHT when Reed and I went out to dinner I felt tired and sick. Over the next few days, I was tired and constipated and a bit nauseous. And then I started spotting. This time it was actually pink. I also felt some scraping in my uterus. Some women feel slight cramping or lower back pain during implantation, but many feel nothing at all. For me, it was like I could feel the fertilized egg burrowing into my uterine wall. I was hopeful that maybe this time I was pregnant, but having been disappointed so many times, I wouldn't get my hopes up. The spotting continued for the next few days and went from brown to red. I started worrying that it was just my period again. I would sometimes have sex to "dislodge" my uterine lining and get my period started if that's what was going to happen. I don't know where I came up with the idea to do this, but sometimes when I was just starting my period, having sex would make it come on faster. In my silent desperation to become pregnant again, this became yet another tool I used to determine if I had implantation bleeding or my period. It would be a bit of a test for me to see if the bleeding picked up after sex or not. I didn't talk to Reed about what I was doing—so much of this struggle was held internally for me. I was so ashamed of my feelings and I just held everything close, running through all the ways I could try to control the outcome in my head. Reed was just happy to be close to me, connecting and intimate.

We were intimate a few times over the next few days, and the bleeding continued, but was light and never really increased. Soon the spotting stopped altogether, and I thought for sure I must be pregnant.

I started obsessing about ham, cheese, and egg sandwiches and ate about three of them in one day. I remember eating one at dinner and was so completely overtaken with how amazing it was, and Reed looked at me and said, "You must be pregnant." The next morning we took a pregnancy test and it was positive!

Reed had continued to be supportive of me while we cycled through months of trying to get pregnant. We had grieved so openly together when the miscarriage first happened. It brought us much closer as a couple, and I saw his strength and his ability to hold me up when I just couldn't bear the weight anymore. As the months wore on, we talked about the fact that we weren't getting pregnant again. I remember telling him that we would have a baby—one way or another. I wouldn't give up, even if it meant adoption. I knew so deeply that I wanted to be a mother, so I had come to terms with the fact that it might not happen in the way I expected. We had many conversations over the months, and on one day in particular I wasn't able to contain my sadness. I had been trying to carry on as normal and hide my pain, but it was always right under the surface, looking for an opening to bubble over the edge. We were sitting on the couch in what would become the baby's room, and I started sobbing. Reed was surprised at the depth of my pain so many months later. He hadn't realized that it was still so raw for me. He held me close, and in that moment, I think he silently agreed to help in whatever way he could to heal my heart and to get pregnant again.

I'm Not Relieved, I'm Terrified... And I Feel Guilty

I expected to feel excited, to feel relieved once I found out I was pregnant again. Instead, I was terrified. There was a moment of feeling happy, but then the fear sank in. *What if it happens again? How do I know it won't?* How would I survive if I lost another baby? I couldn't allow myself to be happy or hopeful because I couldn't bear to have my heart broken again. To love this baby, to accept it, to invest my heart, to open my heart, meant that I could be devastated again. It was just too much.

What no one tells you is that once you become pregnant again, the fear is almost insurmountable. I would cry and cry every day, scared of losing the baby. The range of emotions was overwhelming, and none of them were positive. I was intensely sad from losing the other baby. And in the few moments where I allowed myself to feel a little happy about being pregnant again, I would be overcome with guilt. Guilt at feeling hopeful. Guilt at feeling happy and excited. Naive for allowing myself to think that I might be able to carry this baby to term. Guilt that if this baby did survive, that somehow I had done something more, something better than I had for the baby I lost.

I know now that the fear of losing everything is a normal part of the grieving process after loss. In the case of miscarriage, it is normal to deeply fear losing another baby. It's normal to blame yourself for the loss. For me, this fed into the shame and guilt I felt, and it was compounded when I became pregnant again. There was a part of me that felt like if this baby survived, that somehow I hadn't done enough for the first one. Somehow it was still my fault.

With my first pregnancy, I became connected to my baby instantly. I felt bonded and like our souls were deeply intertwined. With this baby, I didn't feel that right away. I was blinded with fear. The sadness and guilt kept me closed off, and I couldn't connect to my new baby. I wouldn't allow myself to because I was still mourning the one I lost.

Many women have bonding issues with a pregnancy after miscarriage, but again, because of the shroud of silence, no one talks about it. I wasn't warned that I might feel this way—disconnected, scared, and full of shame. I suffered with these feelings in silence. *Here I am, pregnant again after trying desperately for so many months, and I can't even be happy about it. I'm not celebrating it.*

What an awful mother I was. Everyone around me was excited for me. I had moments where I felt that way, but for many months I held this baby at bay, lingering in the chasm, waiting for another unseen force to come and take it away.

If I had admitted that I felt this way, how would society have viewed me? Would I be deemed a terrible mother? Did I love this baby less because I couldn't let myself be excited? Because I couldn't let my heart open up to another possible loss? Pregnant women are supposed to be glowing and excited, not terrified. If I had asked people not to congratulate me, how would they have responded? If we don't recognize the depths of pain in losing a baby to miscarriage, then how can we understand the fear of losing another one?

Bleeding Again

A week after I found out I was pregnant, I started bleeding.

I called the doctor's office and the nurse advised me to lie down and rest. I called back a few hours later and pleaded with them to have my doctor call me back. When she called, I was hysterical. "I'm so scared," I sobbed over the phone. She was so patient and understanding. "Okay," she responded, "Let's look at your hCG number and then we can see whether you are still pregnant or losing the baby." I was shaking and sick and riddled with anxiety.

I went in to have my blood drawn. The next twenty-four hours waiting for the results were excruciating. The hCG test measures the amount of pregnancy hormone in your body; it can be a way to indicate whether you are pregnant and whether you are miscarrying. The number came back good: in the 800s. Not great, but it was an okay number.

My doctor said she couldn't tell me definitively what was happening, but not to be discouraged. I was tested again, and three days later the number had gone up to 3,000. A few days later I went in for an ultrasound.

I was scared when Reed and I went in. We sat in the dark examination room and tried to get a read on what the ultrasound tech saw. She wouldn't give us much of an indication. She did see a yolk sac, the structure that provides nutrients until the placenta forms. But that was it. No heartbeat, and no fetal pole, the first sign of a forming embryo. I was only five weeks and five days pregnant, so that didn't necessarily mean something was wrong. The good news was that it was not an ectopic pregnancy and there was at least something still inside of me. My hCG had gone up to about 9,000, which was another positive sign.

All this time, I was battling my inner demons and emotions. I was so scared. I went to the bathroom constantly to see if I was spotting. I was now obsessed with making sure I would know if something was wrong with the pregnancy and if I was going to lose the baby.

Taking Control

Aside from the emotional trauma of my miscarriage, I had justifiable medical causes for worry. With my history of thyroid issues, I knew I had a legitimate cause for concern. I had my thyroid checked when I found out I was pregnant; this time, the TSH number came back alarmingly high. I was told that this could lead to neurological and developmental issues in the baby if it was not addressed. Thyroid function is critical to the healthy development of a baby's brain. This time around, I was determined to be more aggressive with treatment to try to reduce any potential harm to the baby.

I told my doctor I wanted to ramp up my medication immediately and significantly and that I wanted to be tested again in a week to see whether the change was bringing down my TSH. She advised otherwise, but I made it very clear that what she had suggested wasn't going to cut it this time. I was going to do whatever I had to do to make sure I was doing what I felt was right.

A week later, my TSH had started to come down but still had a ways to go. After another week, it was within normal range. It had worked. I felt like I had really accomplished something by forcing the issue and getting my body back in balance so that I could support my baby's growth and development.

It was the first time I felt like a mother, and I felt a bit of peace about the pregnancy. I had listened to my instincts and they had proven me right—a painful lesson from losing my first baby, but one that made me determined to fight for my child no matter the cost. I had finally stood in the fullness of being a mother—of being my baby's first and foremost caregiver.

There's a Heartbeat

I continued to have cramping and spotting for a week after the first ultrasound. I called in to the office again, crying, and they scheduled me for another ultrasound at what would have been six weeks. Again, the dread and anxiety were overwhelming. Reed and I went in and thankfully we had a different technician to help us. She was much more friendly than the last one. The room was dark, and Reed and I were both visibly nervous. In typical form, Reed made a joke to try to lighten the mood. Thankfully, the technician laughed and seemed to open up to us. I had never been so grateful for Reed's schoolyard humor. My voice shaking, I explained that we were there because I had lost my last baby and was terrified of losing this one.

She began the scan and turned the screen to face us. It's protocol for the technician to simply perform the scan and have a doctor review the results before they offer any indication of viability, but she pointed at the screen and showed us the flicker of the little heartbeat.

"Is that the heartbeat? Oh my God. Thank you." I started crying with relief. So far so good with this little one. Despite the bleeding and worry, this baby was hanging on.

We left feeling some relief, but still bracing ourselves for bad news in the coming weeks. We had seen a strong heartbeat of the baby we lost, so while it was comforting to see it, we knew that things could still go terribly wrong.

I've been asked about what Reed's experience of the miscarriage was and how the months and pregnancy that followed impacted him. As much as I had been failed by the medical community, he too, had been let down. Neither of us had ever expected to lose a baby, so when the doctor told us that our first baby's heartbeat was gone, Reed felt like the roof had caved in. Suddenly everything we had planned for was gone. He says it's the worst thing that has ever happened to him- that moment- realizing what it all means. He hadn't been prepared for how to support me through the miscarriage and grief. Neither of us knew what would happen the night I took the misoprostol. How could we? He spent the next year and a half doing everything he could to support me and try to keep me from the darkness of my grief.

He processed the loss more quickly than I did, and from there, his sole focus became how to support his broken wife. I had many very dark days and he worried about me and my well-being. Once I became pregnant again, he was concerned that my anxiety was not only bad for me, but could also harm the baby. He tended to my every need and showed me strength at every moment—when I couldn't get out of bed, every time I crumbled to the ground in tears. He held my hand, he cradled me as he listened to my sobbing, and he never once allowed me to see his own fear. He made sure we did everything we could to make the second pregnancy successful—whether we had any control of it or not. He had to carry on and be the backbone for both of us. He knew that if I saw even a glimpse of anxiety in him, I would collapse. When we committed to one another above the ocean in Big Sur, I don't think either of us could have imagined the pain we would have to carry on our shoulders— mine for my sweet baby that was gone, and his for the baby he lost and the wife he was trying to save.

Trying to Carry On As Usual

The next week, I started puking in the morning. Most people would say this was a good sign, but since I was throwing up in my last pregnancy, even after the baby had died, it was not reassuring. That week, I had to travel for work. I was dreading the trip and tried to get out of it, but I was in litigation with my company and we were taking a deposition of the plaintiff. I had to be there. I flew to Minneapolis, where it was beyond freezing. I was feeling terrible and was scared about what flying would do to the baby. Normally I would have a glass of wine on the plane to help me relax, but that wasn't an option. I gutted it out, feeling awful, and arrived in the freezing cold.

I had decided to stay near the law firm to simplify the morning, knowing how terrible I felt when I woke up. What I didn't plan for was the fact that I was staying at a tiny, not very nice hotel, and the restaurant was closed when I arrived. I ended up ordering terrible Chinese food and eating fried rice in my room watching TV.

The next morning, I woke up jet-lagged and nauseous. I barfed in the hotel toilet, hovering over the hard, cold floor, and then tried to make myself look presentable. It was still so early in my pregnancy, so I didn't want anyone to know.

That being said, I knew it was going to be hard to hide how awful I felt.

On top of feeling bad, I was having tremendous anxiety about being locked in a conference room for ten hours feeling sick. I had packed every coping tool I could—tea, crackers, mints, gum, and water. I knew if I could get through the morning I would be okay.

Because of this first-trimester silence, I was left to try to hide how I was feeling and carry on like normal. Instead of being offered support and understanding, women have to slip away to the bathroom to throw up or make up excuses for why we need to work from home so many days. We get creative with our explanations in an effort to keep hidden what is happening. All of this because we aren't supposed to acknowledge a growing baby—because we might lose it.

As an attorney, I felt like I had to contort myself to keep up my professional image. I was suffering, anxious, and guilt-ridden—consumed almost every minute with whether I would lose this baby, but I had to sit around a table with other lawyers and pretend that I was aggressive, strong, and unflappable. All the posturing I would normally use in this context went out the window as I just tried to get through the day. And why is that? Why couldn't I be scared and strong? Why couldn't I have told everyone that I had morning sickness but I would still prepare and argue my cases like a heavyweight in the boxing ring? Is that somehow incongruous? If they had known the emotional struggle that was going on inside of me, would they have taken advantage of it? Used it against me or my client? I couldn't let anyone outside my family see me as weak.

The deposition was contentious and opposing counsel and the plaintiff were aggressive and argumentative. It was painful.

I made it through the day and ended up telling the women attorneys I was working with that I was pregnant. It helped to have their support and for them to understand why I was so quiet all morning. We slogged through two days of the deposition and I was finally on my way home. I didn't have anymore spotting on the trip and I was looking forward to getting home and going to our eight-week appointment.

As a pregnant woman, my job and my motherhood were a juggling act. At least that fact is acknowledged in society at large. But as a grieving woman who had miscarried her first child, I discovered society didn't have a place for me.

The Eight-Week Checkup

For this first appointment at our new OB's office, I was seen by a nurse practitioner. Nurse Practitioners are not board-certified doctors, but they have more training than a typical nurse and can perform many of the same exams as a doctor. Our medical group at the new clinic alternated appointments with doctors and NPs. When we went in to meet with the nurse practitioner, she was communicative and warm; she must have noticed how quiet I was. While Reed chatted away with her, I sat there with a plastic smile on my face. She looked at me and said, "You had a miscarriage before. You must be scared. So let's do the ultrasound first and then we can talk about everything else." I don't know if it was that she was well trained in bedside manner or sensitivity protocol or that it was simply her personality, but here, finally, was someone who acknowledged and understood my anxiety.

I teared up with relief. And with fear.

She turned out the lights and went into the hall to grab the ultrasound machine. She wheeled it into the room and again, I had the cold wand inserted. After what felt like forever, she showed us the screen and smiled. A healthy fetus and a strong heartbeat.

We were one step closer to having a healthy baby. I felt relieved, a bit, but also still scared. After all, I had been down this road at my last eight-week appointment. *Everything's fine. Nothing to worry about. There's a strong heartbeat.*

And then nothing. Dead. Empty. I was trying to be optimistic, but it was hard. I had to gut it out, teeth clenched, until the next ultrasound.

Gel on My Stomach Again

I was still spotting, so I booked another doctor's appointment, even though the office typically didn't do another ultrasound until thirteen weeks to check the neuchal translucency and then again at twenty weeks for a full anatomy scan. A clinic would usually only see me at eight weeks and then again at twelve weeks, but I insisted on coming in at ten weeks and begged for an ultrasound. Thankfully the reception staff was incredibly understanding and patient with me and had my doctor call me back. I explained to my doctor that this was when the last baby died and I just couldn't wait another four weeks to find out. The anxiety I was feeling was bad for the baby and my pregnancy, so she let me come in at ten weeks.

I braced myself when she put the cold gel on my stomach. The sensation brought me right back to the last time I had felt it.

When I miscarried and they sent the second doctor in to confirm that the baby was dead, that doctor had squeezed a bunch more gel on my stomach and I remember how cold it felt. She'd pushed hard, searching, as I lay there waiting, desperately hoping she would tell me something different.

I pulled myself out of that memory and looked over at the screen. There was a baby. And it was moving and big. It was okay. My doctor turned on the sound so we could hear the heartbeat again. I was in disbelief.

She took some measurements, confirmed that everything looked on track, and sent us out with some pictures.

Everything looked fine. I began to let myself go a little and felt a flicker of relief. The baby even had a bit of a fist in the air in one of the pictures. My little freedom fighter in there. I exhaled.

Walking out of the office, I expected to feel completely relieved, but I didn't. I felt much better, but I was still bracing myself for bad news. Guarding my heart from being shattered again. I still couldn't allow myself to connect completely with this baby.

It would be much later before I realized why, but in that moment, all I knew was that it was time to bring out the maternity clothes again.

Maternity Clothes Again

I had kept some maternity clothes from the last pregnancy. Wedging myself into my jeans was starting to get painful, so I tried on the grey pants from my first shopping trip. When I saw myself in the mirror in them, I felt sick. I threw them away. I had been so excited about maternity clothes the first time, about being able to show off my growing belly. This time, I just felt apprehensive. It was another sign of what I had lost. But reality set in that I was getting bigger and I'd have to buy more clothes. I wasn't telling people yet, so I needed a few things that would help me hide the fact that I was pregnant and that I could take on our upcoming vacation.

When I went shopping, I couldn't bear to go into the dressing rooms again, so I grabbed some leggings, a pair of shorts and a few shirts, and left. This time, I didn't go into the fancy maternity store for designer jeans and sweaters. Just a few basics. Nothing to celebrate.

The dressing room at the Gap held some of the worst emotions for me. When I was there during my first pregnancy, I was full of excitement and happiness. I was getting to do what I had waited years for—picking out the clothes I would wear as a glowing pregnant woman. I remember looking at myself in the mirror and being so excited. But now the dressing room was the symbol of all that I had lost: the openness, the naivete, the freedom, the baby. My baby was already dead when I bought the maternity clothes, so there I was, staring in the mirror, happy and dreaming about the months to come growing my baby, and all the while she was dead. I felt stupid for being excited. Stupid for not knowing she was dead. Stupid for getting my hopes up.

This type of trauma and post-traumatic stress is surprisingly common. One study by the Imperial College in London showed that as many as 40% of women reported experiencing symptoms of post-traumatic stress disorder after losing a baby to miscarriage. According to the Mayo Clinic, symptoms of PTSD can include flashbacks, nightmares, severe anxiety, and uncontrollable thoughts about the event. Why isn't this talked about more? Why aren't women warned that this might happen? I was experiencing PTSD and had no idea. I suffered for months, the symptoms impacting my work and relationships, yet no help was offered. My first doctor never called to check on me. She never offered information about what to look for or where to find help. Even if I couldn't have heard her in the moments when the grief first set in, shouldn't she have sent some information home with me? Couldn't she have given Reed a brochure, suggested we see a counselor, or offered some resources about how to help me? He was doing his best to wade through this intensely difficult time and to support me, on his own, through my grief. Couldn't she have prepared us for what we would now face as a couple? Why was a doctor still failing to provide us with information we needed at every turn?

Because this is routine for them. But it's not for those of us losing our baby.

Forgiveness

A few weeks after the ten-week ultrasound, I went in for another session with my Chinese Medicine practitioner, Jen. I was going every two weeks, and every time, I would lie on the table and just cry. She would talk me through what I was feeling and help me start to work through my grief. I was overcome with sadness and fear and would replay horrible moments in my head. I would wrack my brain, searching for a sign I must have missed. I couldn't understand why this baby was alive and my other one wasn't. It didn't make any sense. It wasn't fair. I could not let go of the guilt and shame I felt about losing my baby. I knew it was somehow my fault.

I believed that if I had done something differently, I could have saved my baby. If only I had pushed my thyroid doctor the first time around. If only I hadn't taken the antibiotics. If only I had known something was going wrong, I could have saved her. I wasn't a good enough mother to keep her alive. It was my one job to protect her, and I failed.

According to a 2015 study by *Obstetrics and Gynecology*, 47% of survey respondents reported feeling guilty after suffering a miscarriage. How can it be that nearly half of the women who lose a baby will feel responsible for it, yet this isn't widely talked about? Feeling responsible made me question who I was at the deepest levels—made me question whether I was as strong as I thought I was, whether I could ever be a good mother or wife. I thought I was the only one who felt this way. *I've failed my baby. I've failed my husband.* Had I known how common this feeling was, perhaps I could have recovered from it sooner. Would I have been on the table with Jen, weeping over my guilt for months, all the while not bonding with my new baby?

Lying on Jen's table, I thought that if I let myself let go and love this new baby, I would be betraying the one I lost. I would lose her, forget her. I couldn't brush the loss aside or bury it. I had failed her once and I would not allow anyone to forget that she was here, if only for a brief moment. If I loved a new baby, how could I still love her?

I was lying on the table sobbing, unable to breathe, and fighting the love and connection to my new baby. He was pulling at my heart, but I didn't want to allow myself to give in. Jen said to me, while cradling me with her hands on my back and my heart, "*This* baby needs you now. You have to fight for *this* baby."

In that moment, I realized that I *was* a mother. That I had another baby who needed me and that I had to let go. Not of the baby I lost, but of the wall I had put up around my heart. I finally allowed myself to open my heart to this new life being formed. I decided I had to honor the baby that I lost and find a way to open myself up to loving someone else. I had to allow myself to be happy.

A few weeks later, we found out we were having a boy. After that appointment, once I was home and resting, I had a flood of emotion. I had to allow myself to feel this baby, to breathe him, to take care of him, to connect to him. I had to find a way to resolve these feelings of sadness and guilt. Through tears, I heard myself for the first time since losing my baby.

I forgive myself.
For failing you.
For not knowing how to keep you safe.
For not trusting myself when I knew something was wrong.
For not fighting for you.
For not being what you needed me to be.
For not being your mother in the truest sense. My job was to protect you, and I failed.
Please forgive me.

In the midst if my sobs, I suddenly had a vision. I saw a little girl standing next to me while I was lying on my bed. She took my hand and held it, placing both of our hands on my growing belly. She said, "Mama, have my brother first. I promise I will come back to you."

I finally felt at peace.

PART II

Help

What Will I Feel and Experience?

When I first lost the baby, I began to realize after the blinding few weeks that followed that I probably needed help to process what had happened and to heal. I had tried to move on and deal with it on my own, but it was a constant ache that followed me everywhere I went. I felt no joy, no peace, no light. There was only darkness and a few moments where I would forget what had happened. I would be free for a moment, and then the blanket of sadness would once again wash over me. The emotions would overtake me, and I would collapse into tears.

I started by looking for books and resources online. I am not a particularly religious person, so the books that related the loss to God and heaven didn't resonate. Any faith I'd had in the Universe or something bigger had been shaken to its core by my loss. There were a few articles about the medical part of miscarriage, but that didn't make me feel any better. I happened upon a few short essays that I liked, but I was shocked at how little was available. If this happens to nearly an estimated third of known pregnancies, how is there so little support? How is there nothing out there for me to read to understand what would happen to me?

Why didn't I know what to expect?

My doctor had given me no information about what would happen to me physically. Being startled by my water breaking and seeing the dead fetus in the toilet were experiences I was not prepared for. I wish I had been able to read about what would happen to me. I wish someone would have told me what to expect. Instead, I was left to find out, alone, in the dark, water breaking, bleeding, sobbing.

Even if there had been technical medical descriptions of what would happen, there was nothing to prepare me for the emotional toll it would take. No one told me the loss would linger, holding me captive for over a year. No one told me I would still hold on to it, still cry at the thought, five years and two healthy babies later.

One essay talked about going to the hospital for a D&C procedure[2]. The author said, "I went out full and returned empty." That's exactly how I felt. I was full—full of hope, joy, life. And now I was empty. I couldn't fill that emptiness. Not with food, not with alcohol, not with a new baby. I was empty.

I'm Scared

Of the few essays I found that did talk about the feelings of loss, none prepared me for the fact that when I finally did get pregnant again, I would be faced with a whole new set of fears and pain.

The fear paralyzed me. I so desperately wanted to get pregnant again—it was an insatiable need. I thought I would feel

2 "I Went Out Full", Emily Bazelon and Dahlia Lithwick, in *About What Was Lost*

relieved and that relief and joy would somehow replace the emptiness. But when we finally did get pregnant again, I was terrified. I spent nearly every waking moment worrying about losing the baby. Every cramp, every spot of blood or mucus, every time I felt sick or didn't feel sick. Every appointment was met with panic and terror.

There were the countdowns: Make it to eight weeks, see the heartbeat, make it to eleven weeks, make it past the first trimester, make it past the thirteen-week screening, feel the baby move, make it past the twenty-week appointment, feel the baby move every day, make sure it is moving as much as it was yesterday, or this morning, or an hour ago, make it past twenty-eight weeks when the baby can survive outside the womb, make it to thirty-four weeks when the survival rate increases to 98%, make it through the delivery.

It is a horrible way to live. Constant fear, worry, and panic. But because most of us never know why we lose our babies, we can't ever allow ourselves to feel safe. If I had known what happened—that the antibiotics did it, that there was some rare chromosomal issue, that it was my thyroid—*anything*—I would have felt more at ease with my next pregnancy.

But we don't know why women lose babies. We don't know.

So for those of us who are wounded by a pregnancy loss, we are left to suffer with irrepressible fear.

I Feel Like a Failure

I felt embarrassed and unsure what to say or how to tell people that I had miscarried, so for months, I avoided the people who knew I was pregnant. I had gone to a yoga class in the early days of my first pregnancy and was thrilled to be there, to have my newly pregnant body experience the flood of endorphins from a yoga session. When everyone was sitting, eyes closed, the teacher asked for anyone who had an injury or was expecting to let her know. I raised my hand a bit sheepishly, but also with satisfaction. She came over and I whispered in her ear that I was pregnant. She beamed and hugged me. There were some poses that weren't safe for me, so she advised me to make a few adjustments during class.

After I lost the baby, I couldn't bear to go back. I knew I would eventually have to go the studio again, but I just couldn't. Months and months later, I finally did, hoping it would help heal my heart. I knew I had to start facing my fears, and admitting that I had lost the baby was part of that. When I walked in, the instructor hugged me and said hello. I just stood and looked at her, bracing myself. She said, "I remember you telling me something, but now you're not. Are you okay?" It was painful. But I managed to nod yes, that I was okay, and I didn't break down in tears. I got through it.

Admitting that I lost a baby made me feel like a failure. Like something was wrong with me. Carrying around the sadness made me feel even worse. Not only could I not carry a baby, but I couldn't get over it. I was a wreck and that made me feel even more guilty. We don't allow women—or men, for that matter—the space to grieve for a lost baby. It's like a miscarriage doesn't count. It's not real grief. Not real loss.

How Can I Talk About the Unspoken?

The feeling of failure and the expectation that grief doesn't matter is amplified by the way miscarriage is treated. We don't know why most of them happen. We will never know. But for those of us who have lost our child, it's important that we *do* know. The medical community largely doesn't even bother to find out. They don't do the research. They don't do tests. They don't even tell you what to expect. It's hidden. Unspoken.

When something is unspoken, people feel like they can't or shouldn't talk about it, and so they don't. In that silence, fear, guilt, and shame fester and grow. Why shouldn't we talk about it? Because it makes someone feel uncomfortable? Because they don't want to know that I pulled a fetus out of the bowl of the toilet and cried on the floor next to it? Is that too graphic? Too sad? Too scary? Too mysterious? Too uncontrolled? Does it make you feel incompetent because you don't know how to deal with it or how to help? Do you feel helpless? Like a failure?

Well, my pain has been all of those things. And so has the pain of thousands and thousands of women who have lost their babies.

By not talking about miscarriage, we isolate husbands and partners, friends and families who desperately need their own support or want to know how to comfort a loved one. They can't know how to help because they don't really know what is going on. The depths of pain and sadness are understood only by the silent army of us who have been through it. We carry the secret with a look, with a comforting nod; not saying it out loud, but carrying on as a village of the one in four women who have experienced losing a baby.

We need to talk about it.

We need men and women to know what could happen. And if the worst does, if you are facing losing your baby before you see its face, you need to know what to expect. Physically and emotionally. By not talking about it, we leave women and men unprepared for what could happen. Being blindsided by such a horrifying tragedy leaves a scar that could have been made smaller by just knowing what to expect, how to heal, and where to go for help.

Reed and I both still cry when we talk about what happened. Neither of us knew what to expect. We weren't able to handle the loss and grief gracefully—as gracefully as one might be able to with such a tragic loss. We both retreated to our default of masking pain and of isolation. We didn't know what we were dealing with. How many marriages have been unable to withstand that pain? How many partnerships could be saved by simply providing information, tools, and support for what to expect through the process of losing a baby? By helping couples and families understand that all of this is normal and that it's possible to get through it?

There is a considerable need for better support for those of us who experience this type of loss. Take the shame out of it. Take the secrecy out of it. Miscarriage is a widespread experience with its own indelible process of grief and recovery. Every mother and father has specific and valid needs to help move through that experience, and we shouldn't have to also bear the burden of misinformation and taboo that currently surrounds it.

Who Am I If I Can't Have a Baby?

Losing the baby made me question everything about myself. Everything I thought I was and was supposed to be just didn't make sense anymore.

I thought I was the strongest woman. A fighter. I've been through hardship and struggle before, and I thought, *There's no way I can't do this—no way I can't carry a baby.*

And then I couldn't.

What did it mean to my womanhood when I couldn't keep a baby alive? What did that make me? I clung to my work identity and leaned into it as hard as I could. It was mostly out of desperation, but it helped me feel a bit more human again. I needed to know there was at least one part of me that I wasn't wrong about, one part I hadn't been so painfully mistaken about. It is incredibly difficult to question every single part of yourself, to look in the mirror and not recognize who you are, and part of what is so awful is that you are expected to walk around like nothing ever happened. Especially if it happened in that shrouded "first trimester" where it supposedly doesn't really count anyway.

So I went to work. I got in the car, drove to the office, sat in my chair, got on calls, reviewed emails, paperwork, whatever. I never talked about it to anyone around me: not the person working next to me, not the gal at the checkout line of the grocery store. "How's your day going?" *It's completely gut-wrenching. I'm still bleeding. There's a woman behind me in line cooing at her baby, and I feel like I need to run out of here because listening to it is unbearable.*

I didn't anticipate the impact my miscarriage would have on my sense of self. I certainly wasn't informed by a doctor or medical professional that I might question myself and my identity so deeply. I felt like I was a mother—I had held a baby in my womb—and yet society was telling me that I wasn't. There's no word for a woman who was pregnant and lost her baby.

Was I a mother?

I look around me sometimes and wonder how many silent struggles are going on. How many women are struggling with that exact question right now? Is the woman next to me grieving the same loss I've experienced? How many years have gone by since she lost her baby? Is she still sad? Does she think about her baby as much as I do? Did she ever find out why? Did it give her peace? Does she still cry silently in the bathroom when she gets overwhelmed by the loss? Does she tell her husband, her partner, her mom… anyone? Or does it not bother her at all anymore? Is it just a part of her past that she has somehow reconciled? How did she ever get there?

Let's stop the standard of suffering in silence. Let's allow one another to talk about it. To grieve openly. To be honest about how we're feeling. Isn't it better if people know I am grieving so they understand why I am unable to hold a conversation or carry on as usual?

How Do I Talk About My Grief?

For a long time, I didn't talk much about my miscarriage to other women who I knew had also experienced one unless I knew that I lost my baby later into my pregnancy than they did. I felt like I didn't deserve to be allowed to admit the pain and sadness if I thought theirs was bigger. I felt like they would hear my experience and minimize it in comparison to what they went through. I never felt that way towards the women I know who lost their babies at an earlier stage, but I never wanted to belittle the experience of those who were further along by talking about my grief.

I carried this around with me for years, not wanting to hurt anyone by talking about my pain and holding onto the fear that some people's pain was worse than mine was. But recently, I heard the author and healer Iyanla Vanzant say, "It's not about measuring pain."

This resonated with me. It's *not* about measuring pain. Mine matters just as much as someone who had a stillborn baby. And the woman who lost her baby at week four feels as much pain as I do. As much as all of us do.

A baby that is wanted, hoped for, longed for, is a piece of your soul from the moment you decide to conceive it. I loved my baby long before I was pregnant, and I will continue to love her for the rest of my life. It was the idea of her, the idea of motherhood, the possibility of who she was and who she would become. And of who she would make me. All of that hope and possibility was wrapped up in her, and I would have been devastated if I had lost her at *any* moment. She was a part of my soul, and losing her has left a deep wound.

Imagine the depths of the collective pain of the hundreds of thousands of women who carry this universal experience. We are all grieving. We are here, but unseen. Part of us is gone, shrouded in cultural expectations of dismissal and diminishment of miscarriages. Our pain remains largely unseen, unheard, and unacknowledged, and I am unwilling to participate in that any longer.

I'll start with a step towards healing the collective wound with the same step that helped me towards healing my own.

Imagine what could come of simply asking a woman about her loss. *Recognition* is the first step.

Recognition

In the minutes, days, and weeks that followed my miscarriage, I received lots of love and support from friends and family. Some knew just what to say. Others tore my heart out with their words because our society doesn't openly talk about miscarriage and they didn't know what to say. There isn't a playbook for how to respond when someone tells you they lost a pregnancy.

How Can I Grieve Someone I Never Met?

It is often hard for people to understand that we can grieve and feel a tremendous loss for a baby that was never alive outside of our womb. This idea that emotionally we are supposed to keep the baby growing inside our body at arm's length until twelve weeks is hurting mothers and fathers. For those of us who broke the unspoken rules and loved our baby at the onset, before the second trimester, we are made to feel foolish for doing so. The aftermath was hurt, shame, and grief in a cultural vacuum of misinformation, dismissal, and taboo. Why should I feel ashamed for loving my baby before I knew it was viable? Why should I feel ashamed for being vulnerable and for envisioning my life with that precious new baby?

I believe most people are well meaning and want to provide comfort or hope, but that what they say or do often just doesn't help, and can hurt instead. The response "Well, at least you know you can get pregnant" didn't help. I still didn't have a baby in my arms. I was still empty. "You can try again." "There's always a risk in the first trimester." "At least it happened early." None of this helped me. It was the hope of a baby, a promise that I loved, and it is gone. Nothing can really make it better.

Parents do so much to prepare for the journey they are about to go on: They buy the clothes, look at the baby gear, pick out names, stock up on sparkling water, dream about what they will do with this baby. And then in one moment, it is ripped away and they suddenly feel stupid for doing all of that. Stupid for getting their hopes up. And I imagine, if they allow themselves to feel excited again and the next baby is lost, too, it feels devastating to again have those hopes dashed. The internal dialogue is relentless. *I should have known better. We should have known better.* Being told that it's common in the first trimester just amplifies the feelings of grief, trauma, shame, and guilt.

Some people tried to focus on a spiritual or medical explanation. "It was God's plan," or "The baby must have had chromosomal issues and probably wouldn't have survived." These reasons might help some people feel better, but for me, because I didn't know why my baby didn't survive, it made me angry. What if it wasn't God's plan? What if my doctor or I made a mistake? I wanted to regain a sense of control, and hearing expressions of things I couldn't control only made me feel worse.

In hindsight, the most harmful statements were all rooted in the current climate of misinformation, lack of information, and dismissal. We live in a culture that doesn't understand the details or depth of loss caused by miscarriage for an expecting mother and her family. In an attempt to make things easier for a grieving mother, we brush it aside and try to prop her up with hope and paternalistic explanations. There is clearly a need for more training for medical practitioners, more recognition that a baby lost to miscarriage is a loss, and more open dialogue about what to expect and how to heal. We need more of what helps, not what harms.

What Will Help Me Get Through This?

After she found out about my miscarriage, my friend Heather and her husband sent me a huge bouquet of flowers with a very sweet card that simply read, "We are sorry for your loss." I don't know that most people would think to do that, but it helped me feel better. I needed people to acknowledge that I'd had a baby, and that it was now gone. It was a loss. A death. I needed to grieve and I needed people to support me in that process. Ignoring what happened, downplaying it, brushing it off, or trying to force me to focus on the positive or what was possible in the future set back my healing. It made me feel like I had to justify that I was grieving and explain that this was a baby to me, that it was a real loss, and I deserved the space to feel sad, and angry, and confused. What helped was when family and friends offered acknowledgment, supportive gestures, and space for healing without explanations.

Grief is a very personal experience. What I needed may very well be different than what someone else needs. What provided comfort to me might not resonate with someone else. Grief is personal, but it is also universal. We all will experience it at some time. There are tools and support networks that can help people process various types of grief and loss, and I've included some of those resources at the end of this book. There are ways to work with mothers who have experienced post-traumatic stress like I did.

As a society, a willingness to acknowledge the loss of a pregnancy as a very real need for grief and recovery would begin to allow us to provide better information and sensitivity, as well as open the door to the care and support that women and families need.

How Can I Work While Grieving?

Perhaps nowhere else did I feel the cultural shroud of taboo and secrecy around miscarriage as strongly as I did at work. I worked in a male-dominated industry, at a male-dominated company, and there wasn't really anywhere to turn to get support. These were not the Mark Zuckerbergs of grief. These were awkward, cold, all-about-business guys. They would not have known how to handle what I would tell them, so I kept it to myself. Plus, I was the head of HR, so there wasn't anyone else to go to talk to about my "feelings." As a lawyer, I had to keep up my appearance as a strong, tough-as-nails, take-no-BS leader at the company.

Sobbing in the bathroom stall would have put my professional image in question, and at that moment, it felt like that's all I had left. I didn't know who I was anymore, but at least I knew I was still good at my job. I'm sure my work suffered at times, but at other times, it was the only thing that could take my mind off the pain for a few minutes.

Thankfully I had an office with a door, so when I felt the tears well up, I could walk over and close it until I could pull myself together. The memory of getting on a conference call an hour after I found out my baby had died remains sharp in my mind. I felt obligated to carry on like everything was normal—because as far as everyone around me at work was concerned, it was. No one knew I was pregnant, so no one knew I was going through a miscarriage. One of my biggest regrets in this process is that I dialed into that conference call. It dishonored my grief. It dishonored my baby. But because I hadn't told anyone, I didn't know how to tell my boss moments before an important call that I couldn't dial in. I should have been able to talk about it, and to take the time I needed to process what I was experiencing. How many women carry on, bleeding through pads during meetings or making up excuses for why they can't come in to work, silently hiding the very real, very tragic loss they are experiencing?

Having to work while grieving is a difficult position for women to be in, let alone mothers who have recently endured the loss of a child and might be recovering from trauma. It would be helpful to have workplace policies that more clearly support taking time off to grieve the loss of a baby by miscarriage or stillbirth—policies that allow a woman the space and flexibility to decide whether continuing to work is beneficial for her or not. Recovery is not only physical, but mental and emotional. Men and partners need to be able to take time off for their own grief and to support their partners or families in managing theirs. Many women need the time and resources to turn to a therapist or counselor as they process what has happened, and others will want to return to work to help them heal. It should be a choice that grieving people are free to make for themselves.

The process of recovery won't be the same for every woman or man, but lack of information and ignoring the very real grief of miscarriage in the workplace—whether among those in grief or among employees and coworkers—can no longer be standard protocol.

How Can I Manage My Fear If I Conceive Again?

My pregnancy with my first son, Wyatt, after the miscarriage was excruciatingly anxiety-ridden. By the time I became pregnant with my second son, Hudson, I was a little less scared, but it was in part because I had a toddler to chase around whose needs distracted me from the worry and fear. I didn't share how scared I was with many people—only with Reed and with Jen during my craniosacral sessions. It would have been comforting to know that my fear was normal—that I wasn't a terrible mother for wanting to guard my heart. It would have been helpful to know that other women felt that way, that my reaction to my pregnancies after miscarriage was normal.

I now understand too deeply that I not only experienced the loss of a baby, but also the loss of a dream and of innocence in my expectations as a mother. I lost the excitement and joy over every pregnancy that followed. Fear, guilt, and mistrust took their place and I had to fight to allow myself to be excited and invested in these new babies before they were born. That distance, a natural way to protect myself, became yet another source of shame and guilt.

I was scared of the pain of losing another pregnancy, and I was afraid of society's judgment of me as somehow naive for loving a baby that hadn't yet been born, particularly if it was during the first trimester. If we remove the shame and stigma around loving an unborn baby, *even in the first trimester*, then perhaps women and men will feel more open to allowing themselves to invest in a subsequent pregnancy.

We should want to keep our hearts open, even if it's hard or scary, and even if we risk the fragility and power of grief, as love always does. And what greater love is there than that of a parent to a child? The depths of love for a child bring with it the most immense joy, but also the potential for devastating loss. The choice to openly accept this dichotomy is the essence of becoming a parent.

She Made Me a Mother

As I write this, I am sitting in a hotel room in Carmel, a few blocks away from the hotel where I lay in the fetal position for hours on end. Blocks away from the beach where I watched the sunset with Reed and didn't know if I would ever catch my breath again. I still cry when I think about it. The knot fills my stomach and my eyes well up, even though one of my babies, Hudson, now lies asleep in the room next to me. The loss of my first baby wasn't filled by more children.

You can't replace what was lost.

But it does help to have a warm neck to settle into. To have a soft cheek pressed against mine. To feel little hands and little feet. The sweaty head resting on my arm in deep slumber. I have somewhere to turn for love. For happiness. I will always miss my first child, *her*. But I now have two sweet babies, two sons, who light up my life and give me purpose.

Wyatt, my oldest son, is deeply intuitive, wild and intellectual—always asking to understand the written and unwritten rules of life, even at a very young age. He tells me frequently that he remembers being inside my "cave" and tears up when he talks about remembering being born because he was so happy to finally get to see me. While the scientific community hasn't yet validated these types of prebirth memories, much about memory remains a mystery and the detail and emotion with which Wyatt talks about these memories make them seem very real. It stunned me the first time he talked about it, and it brought me to tears, imagining that perhaps, too, my sweet little girl remembered being inside of me.

One day when he was three, Wyatt and I were looking at old photos of our wedding. He asked, "Mommy, where was I that day?" Without thinking, I responded, "You were there, baby. You were just still in my heart." That completely satisfied him. He could understand the concept that he has always existed to me. He has always been there, in my heart. Even when he was just a thought, an idea, a hope—when he was still a seed somewhere in the realm of love, waiting to bloom.

I now use that idea to talk about loved ones lost. It has made some of those discussions less painful than I imagined. When my beloved dog passed away, I dreaded telling Wyatt. I was afraid that his grief would mirror the depths that mine had gone to. But I explained to him that we couldn't see her anymore and that she would live only in our hearts now. He simply asked who would feed her, and then moved on, completely understanding the concept that there is a continuum of life, but love never goes away. Even now, when we talk about my life as a little girl, looking at photos of the lilacs and roses from my childhood garden, he will say, "Oh, when I was in your heart."

When Wyatt was first handed to me, moments after he was born, my soul recognized his. I knew in that moment that we had always been together—it was his sweet soul that lived in my heart as a little girl. I knew that I had been waiting for him for the years that I dreamt of being a mother and the months that I carried him in my body, but when I saw and smelled him for the first time, I knew that I had known him my entire life. He had been a part of me, even when I didn't know it. In that moment, I knew that my baby girl had always been there, too, and that she would always be.

Miscarriage taught me the deepest truth about love: It always carries risk, but it always carries beauty, even if it's buried deep beneath the soil. Like seeds or flower buds not yet ready to blossom, my babies were always in my heart, growing and waiting for the sunlight to bring them forth.

Losing my first baby made me a mother in the truest sense. With her, I didn't advocate for myself and my pregnancy enough. I didn't listen to my instincts enough. I let other people tell me what to do and what was right. Now, as a mother, I follow my intuition. I don't worry too much about what other people think I should do. I will always advocate for my children and stand up for them. As children, these souls have been entrusted to me—I am their sun, their soil, their shelter from the storm. I am the roots that hold them up and from which they can grow into their fullest beauty, strong and wild.

I don't know if anything I could have done would have created a different outcome for myself and my first baby, but I do know I would have felt better knowing that I had done everything I could, just as I was able to for Wyatt and Hudson. During my first pregnancy, I didn't push hard when my instincts as a mother told me to do something differently than what was being advised by my doctor. And I didn't know enough to understand that someone else, a doctor, could be making decisions that could put my pregnancy at risk. I considered my doctor the expert of my own pregnancy, not me. This was a painful lesson to learn.

The hard beauty in the loss of my first baby gave me the gift of urgency, of gratitude, and in some ways, of healthy fear and healthy love for my following pregnancies and my boys. I didn't take my second and third pregnancies for granted and I don't take a second for granted with my boys now. It doesn't make the moments where I'm mad or tired or frustrated disappear. But it does give me pause when I start to worry about the little things in parenting. I know too well how close a devastating loss could be—at times it still feels palpable—and because of that, I do my best to make sure that every moment is filled with love and that they never go to sleep without hearing "Mommy loves you."

I am the first to admit that I still experience the ongoing aftermath of loss; I am fearful of losing my sons because I know the thorns of pain and loss, the scars they leave afterward. But this same awareness also pushes me to stay loving, to stay open, to keep growing and to remain vulnerable.

What is there if we don't risk everything for love?

WHERE DO WE GO FROM HERE?

I HAVE BEEN asked why I chose to write this book. Why would I want to relive the pain and talk about such deeply personal experiences? When it happened to me, I felt alone and I was scared. Despite this being a taboo topic, I hope that in sharing my story, women and men might have somewhere to turn for more help, information and comfort. Just as I so desperately needed all of these things for myself.

Where do we go from here?

When I first was pregnant, I didn't know how common it was to miscarry. I was completely unprepared for what happened to me. Once I got through the actual experience of it, I didn't find much support for what I was going through, both during the actual miscarriage and in the emotional aftermath—a period that lasted for a year and a half.

I needed to know what would happen to my body. I needed to talk about it. I needed to feel like I wasn't alone, but at the time, I felt like the only woman in the world who was going through it. No one prepared me, and when I looked for help,

I found very little. This has begun to change in recent years as many courageous women and men have come out to tell their stories, but more is still needed. I couldn't find what I needed; not in my community, not online, not in bookstores. My friends and family didn't know how to support me because most of them hadn't experienced a loss like this. They did their best, and it is because of them that I survived. But I don't want women to feel like I did—alone, scared, confused, guilty, and drowning.

I want parents to be prepared for the possibility of a miscarriage so when they are told that all the signs show a normal progression, that might not be the case. You can lose a baby at any time in your pregnancy. While admitting that is terrifying, we can all benefit from understanding it to be true and knowing which signs to watch for and steps to take. Knowing what could happen and how to process it emotionally and physically would have made my experience easier. That way, we can prepare to some degree and have a support system in place if the worst happens. And it will happen to about a third of us.

I want people to know exactly what happens when you miscarry. I can only speak to my experience, so my hope is that women share their stories on our website so that other women can read about what it's like to have a D&C or a sudden miscarriage. The details are graphic, but I would have been better prepared and less scared if I had known what was going to happen.

While there is some literature and support for both the physical and emotional toll that it takes, I didn't understand beyond vague descriptions of "sadness" and "depression" what I would feel moments, days, and months later. Many women experience actual postpartum depression after losing a pregnancy. Can you imagine going through postpartum depression or the baby blues without a baby? Combine those hormonal fluctuations with the fear and sadness of loss, and we have doomed women to a deep, dark hole. As physically unprepared as I was, the emotional toll was far more than I could have imagined. It's important to know what to expect—what's normal—and that it's possible to get through it.

I hope to shine a light onto the deep, dark taboo that is miscarriage. No one likes to talk about dead babies. No one wants to discuss the fact that many women and families will lose a baby during pregnancy. It's scary and it's sad.

What's equally terrifying is that in most cases we have no idea why a miscarriage is occurring. Can you imagine any other medical issue going largely undiagnosed for so many years? It just wouldn't happen. Miscarriage is brushed under the rug as a "normal" part of childbearing.

We need to be interested in the causes of miscarriage. These are little lives. Little hopes and dreams for parents who desperately wanted them. They matter. Why they died matters. Imagine if we could spare parents from the pain of losing a pregnancy by finding out how to prevent it. We may never know all the reasons a fetus stops growing, but if we learn enough to prevent even a fraction of miscarriages, isn't it worth it? Imagine another disease killing 30-50% of all people who contract it. Wouldn't we be desperate to find a way to reduce that rate? Even by a few percentage points?

We wouldn't stand for that kind of uncertainty with any other medical issue. We would be raising millions of dollars to find a cure. Pouring resources into research. We don't because we've been made to believe those lives don't matter. How a woman or her family feels about this loss doesn't seem to matter. The loss of a child, of motherhood, is not considered a significant medical or clinical situation. If that baby was loved and wanted, shouldn't we want to find out the cause of death and miscarriage? Shouldn't we be given the choice to find out?

It's too scary a topic for most people to internalize, but we need to talk about it. Openly. Honestly. Share our stories so we don't feel alone when we go through it.

No one wrote a "What to Expect When You Miscarry" book, but they should. Women should be given the full range of information about miscarriage and infant loss and told about alternate methods of care. Let's discuss the different options and provide women and families with the information they need to make informed choices about how to manage their pregnancy.

Until we start talking about miscarriage—and normalizing it—women and men will continue to feel isolated and suffer in silence. I'm still wounded by my experience. Being so unprepared. The scars don't disappear, but they do fade.

I have found peace in talking about my experience and finding meaning in the loss of my sweet baby. I wouldn't let her life be for nothing. I wouldn't let her loss be for nothing. There had to be a reason for it. I've also found comfort in talking to other women about their experiences and helping them get through it. When a woman I know experienced a miscarriage recently, I treated her how I had wanted to be treated. We were out for drinks with a bunch of other women and when she shared her story, many of them turned away or said, "I'm sorry," and moved on to another conversation. I hugged her and asked questions, letting her talk, cry, and grieve. If we can validate another woman's experience with more empathy and knowledge, could we turn the tide on the silent suffering?

HOPE: IN THE END IS
THE BEGINNING

I HAD TO find a way to make my loss mean something. I didn't want it to forever be seared into my heart that this was only loss. I wanted to find a way to honor my baby by learning something from the experience, by gaining something from it. Her presence in my life was not just about experiencing pain; it gave me something, too. I have shared how I don't take moments with my children for granted. I have learned to advocate for myself and my babies. And I hope that by sharing my story, I am also beginning to advocate for others who experience this loss. In finding meaning in her loss, I began to find hope again.

My grandmother was a painter, and she would paint flowers and gardens, beautifully washing the canvas with watercolors. When she passed, my mother went through her garage and found rows and rows of paintings, many of which were a work in progress. One was a picture of a flower in late bloom and a seed, not yet open, but rooted. My grandmother had sketched in pencil, *In the end is the beginning*. In the death of the flower, the petals falling off, a seed was born and from it new life was created.

A few months after Wyatt was born, my mom gave me the framed painting for my birthday. I remember feeling stunned at how deeply my grandmother's words spoke to me. Perhaps she, too, had suffered a loss, and had sketched and painted to try to find the golden thread that holds us all together.

In recovery, we learn to find meaning in our loss. We may discover that our risk for love will always be met with hope. In the end, in the death of my sweet baby, I was given the beginnings of motherhood—a seed was planted within me, and from it, my identity as a woman and a mother has grown.

AFTERWORD

IN MY DARKEST days I was so numb I didn't think I would ever feel hope again. Didn't think I would ever feel joy. Ever fill the void that she left. I had a small bit of hope that when I became pregnant again it would wash away the sadness and emptiness and fill it with something else. When it didn't, I began to worry that I would never be able to move on. That even a new baby wouldn't be enough. That I would never be enough.

I didn't know if I would ever feel pure abandoned happiness again.

But I did. And if nothing else, this is what I want you to take away from this book—You will feel happy again. You will experience moments of complete unbridled joy. You were a mother, even if for a brief moment, and you didn't do anything wrong. You deserve to be happy again. It's okay to let yourself.

When I finally held Wyatt for the first time, my world turned to color again. My entire existence changed in that instant. I saw him and knew that I was his mother—I was here to love him and protect him and give him everything in life that he deserves. And in being given that great responsibility, I was finally free to let go.

I was now obligated to love unconditionally and with my whole heart. He deserved a mommy who could look at him and love him freely, no reservations, no fear. I couldn't hold back anymore, couldn't allow myself to be drowned in fear, because loving him meant offering my fullest self. It meant being more. Loving him meant being free.

And in that, I finally found peace. I finally found true happiness again.

For any woman, whatever her recovery and grief may encompass, I truly believe that life wouldn't give us this experience without also giving us a way to overcome it and find hope again. In the end is the beginning—if we can embrace our ability to love, and offer ourselves freely into the world, we can find our way to a new beginning.

Months after I lost my baby, my mom gave me a lilac bush to plant to remember her. The sweet smell of lilac blossoms fill my memories of summer and have become the symbol of the happiest memories of my childhood—of innocence and pure joy. My mom and I had never spoken about the lilacs and how meaningful they were to me, but she knew they were my favorite. Once again, a mother's intuition knew just what her baby needed—she knew I needed to stay connected to my daughter and to honor her memory. I never wanted to forget that I held my little girl, if only for a few weeks, in my body, as her mother. The lilacs would remind me of how strong she was, of how strong *I* was, and that we were both still here, connected by the invisible ties of motherhood. For years, I watered it and dug it up, moved it from house to house, yard to yard.

And this year, five years later, it is finally beginning to bloom.

Resources

American Pregnancy Association:
http://americanpregnancy.org

Office on Women's Health Helpline:
800-994-9662 https://www.womenshealth.gov

Miscarriage Association:
https://www.miscarriageassociation.org.uk

Find a Local Grief Counselor:
https://aihcp.net/american-academy-of-grief-counseling/

Parents Magazine:
"Emotional Aftermath of Miscarriage"

Miscarriage:
A Guide

QUESTIONS WE SHOULD BE ASKING

- In the book, the author shares her deep desire to have children. Do you think most people are intentional about wanting and having children? How do you think desire impacts a mother's connection to her child or pregnancy? How does desire impact her loss of a baby through miscarriage?

- When do you think a woman becomes a mother? What should we call a woman who has lost a baby to miscarriage?

- Whether a mother desires her baby or not, what is the general narrative about miscarriage in our society today? Why don't we like to talk about miscarriage and dead babies? What fears or taboos does this issue raise for you or others?

- The author shares how she was advised to wait on

an ultrasound, and later demanded an ultrasound earlier than recommended. Do you agree with the medical policy for waiting to confirm a pregnancy with an ultrasound? Do you think waiting this long helps or hurts women?

- How might the current policy on waiting periods for medical confirmation impact the silence and taboo around miscarriage?

- Do you think a woman's grief of losing a baby through miscarriage is different if she has or has not had an ultrasound or heard a heartbeat?

- Do you think a woman's experience of losing a baby through miscarriage would be different if ultrasounds were performed earlier?

- Is there any truth to the idea that the medical community might want to suppress attachment to a baby that might die? If so, who do you think benefits from this?

- Did the way the author found out about her miscarriage feel inhumane? How could the process have been better?

- Should there be better protocols of providing women and their partners or support persons with specific information about what to expect during a miscarriage both physically and emotionally? Should they be given resources for emotional support? Should doctors be required to follow up on the mental health of a woman who has miscarried?

- What can families, friends or partners do to better support those experiencing a miscarriage? How can we help get educate those who want to offer support the information and resources to do so?

- Think of all the ways the author felt failed or dismissed during the process of her miscarriage and aftercare. What does her experience say about today's culture around miscarriage within our society and the medical profession?

- Women who lose a baby often go through the stages of grief. In what ways are the stages of grief over miscarriage similar or different than grief from another event or trauma?

- Women who lose a baby to miscarriage often experience this loss in isolation. In her bathroom, her bedroom, or another private or even public situation. How might this experience compound her grief?

- Do you think women should be given better information or precedents about how to honor the child or hope they are losing? How do you think that choice would impact the woman's experience and ability to recover and heal?

- Imagine another disease killing 30-50% of all

people who contract it. Wouldn't we be desperate to find a cure? A way to reduce that rate? These are the stats for miscarriages in pregnancy. Why do you think there isn't much medical research or medical explanation for miscarriages today? Why do you think most miscarriages go undiagnosed?

- In the book, we learn how much fear and anxiety played a role in the author's second pregnancy. Should there be a different medical protocol for a woman who has experienced a miscarriage? More ultrasounds and check ups to help ease any anxiety she may be feeling? How can we better support a woman who is pregnant again after a miscarriage?

- The author discusses not feeling connected to her second baby because of the fear and anxiety she felt. How do you think society views a woman who doesn't display the "appropriate" excitement for a pregnancy after miscarriage? How can we better support women through this process?

- Why do you think guilt and shame play a significant role in this author's miscarriage? Do you think this response is universally shared by women who have miscarried?

- In the chapter "Recognition," the author acknowledges some people's responses to her miscarriage "tore my heart out with their words." How can we best provide verbal and emotional support for women who have miscarried?

- The author comes to terms with her professional reality as a grieving mother while working in a male-dominated industry in this same chapter, and gives us a hard look: How can women's miscarriages be given proper space and respect in the workplace?

- How can we make miscarriage a topic that is more widely discussed? How can we reach more mothers and their families who have experienced the grief of miscarriage and change the way society views this issue?

Acknowledgments

To my sweet baby girl, without you I wouldn't know love and pain as deeply as I do. Without you, I wouldn't see the world in color. Your life and loss have made me a better mother. You have inspired me to pursue a long-held dream- of being an author. I miss you and can't wait to see you again.

To Wyatt and Hudson- My loves. Your lives are an inspiration to me. Seeing your sweet faces everyday is everything I ever wanted. I hope that I have made a life and work that you can be proud of one day. I am so grateful to be your mommy.

To Reed- I would not still be standing without you. Thank you for your love and support. Thank you for letting me sneak away all those mornings to work on this book. You knew how important it was for me to tell my story. I couldn't have juggled it all without you, and I couldn't have gotten through my grief without your willingness to love me through some very dark days. Thank you for being here to celebrate all of the bright days to come.

To Mom, Dad, and Ryan- Your unwavering love and support have made me who I am. You have made me strong enough to speak out about my pain, raise awareness of a system that is broken and to pursue my dreams- even of being a writer. There is no way to ever thank you enough for what you've given me. You've always seen me for who I am, and that has allowed me to see myself.

To Riley- Having you to love through my pain was such an incredible gift. Thank you for being a part of my life and allowing me to get my first glimpse of motherhood.

To My Friends and Family- Tinina, Sienna, Grayson, my dear friends and other family, I am so grateful for your support and encouragement. I appreciate your perspectives, insight and love.

To My Editor Sunny- We found one another through the magical ties that connect all of us in life. You truly have a gift- you could see my story, even when it wasn't clear to me. I came to you with what I thought was a finished work, and you pulled every thread, every emotion, every breath out of me. You have given me a book that I am so proud of. I am honored to have worked with you and to have had your support.

To Meghan at My Two Cents Editing: Thank you for your immaculate eye for editing. Your guidance and support have been invaluable.

To the Women who came before me and to those who will come after me;

To the Brave Women who have shared their stories, and to those who couldn't;

You have inspired me to share mine. These stories need to be told, and I knew that if I could, I had an obligation to. Never stop telling your truth. Never dismiss your pain. Know that you are seen, and that you are not alone.

Made in the USA
Middletown, DE
23 March 2022

63107969R00080